T0358276

ROUTLEDGE LIBRARY EDITIONS: FOOD SUPPLY AND POLICY

Volume 5

BRITAIN'S FOOD SUPPLIES

BRITAIN'S FOOD SUPPLIES

K. G. FENELON

Routledge
Taylor & Francis Group

LONDON AND NEW YORK

First published in 1952 by Methuen

This edition first published in 2020
by Routledge
4 Park Square, Milton Park, Abingdon, Oxon OX14 4RN

and by Routledge
605 Third Avenue, New York, NY 10017

Routledge is an imprint of the Taylor & Francis Group, an informa business

© 1952 K. G. Fenelon

All rights reserved. No part of this book may be reprinted or reproduced or utilised in any form or by any electronic, mechanical, or other means, now known or hereafter invented, including photocopying and recording, or in any information storage or retrieval system, without permission in writing from the publishers.

Trademark notice: Product or corporate names may be trademarks or registered trademarks, and are used only for identification and explanation without intent to infringe.

British Library Cataloguing in Publication Data
A catalogue record for this book is available from the British Library

ISBN: 978-0-367-26640-0 (Set)
ISBN: 978-0-429-29433-4 (Set) (ebk)
ISBN: 978-0-367-27575-4 (Volume 5) (hbk)
ISBN: 978-0-429-29674-1 (Volume 5) (ebk)

Publisher's Note
The publisher has gone to great lengths to ensure the quality of this reprint but points out that some imperfections in the original copies may be apparent.

Disclaimer
The publisher has made every effort to trace copyright holders and would welcome correspondence from those they have been unable to trace.

BRITAIN'S FOOD SUPPLIES

by

K. G. FENELON
M.A., Ph.D.

METHUEN & CO., LTD., LONDON
36 Essex Street, Strand, W.C.2

First published in 1952

CATALOGUE NO. 5395/U

PRINTED IN GREAT BRITAIN

Preface

In this book, the term "food supplies" has been interpreted in a wide sense so as to cover supplies entering the household and consumed by individuals as well as in the broader sense of food supplies leaving the farm or entering the ports. As the preparation of the manuscript progressed, it seemed necessary to widen its scope still further by reference to the world food situation. Britain depends on overseas supplies for a great proportion of her requirements, and the arguments, therefore, would have been incomplete without some reference to the wider aspects of the problem. The book as a whole is largely based on a statistical study of the problems, but in order to avoid over-loading the text with figures, many of the tables have been relegated to an Appendix.

The work had its origin in two papers prepared while I was Director of Statistics and Intelligence at the Ministry of Food, and read before the British Association for the Advancement of Science at the Newcastle (1949) and the Birmingham (1950) Meetings. They were subsequently published by the Association in its Journal, *The Advancement of Science*.

As will be evident from the context, the book was written before I took up my present appointment as Government Statistician in Iraq, but owing to inevitable delays in printing, it was not possible to publish it before I left for Baghdad. I have endeavoured to bring references and tables as far as possible up-to-date, though distance from libraries and other sources has made this task somewhat more difficult than it would have been at home. I hope, however, that any shortcomings in this direction have, at least in part, been offset by the greater detachment with which I was able to revise the proofs after twelve months' residence in the Middle East.

I would take this opportunity of thanking all those friends, who, directly or indirectly, have helped me in the preparation

v

of the book and in particular my thanks are due to former colleagues at the Ministry of Food. I am indebted to the Librarians of the Ministry of Food and the Royal Statistical Society for their unfailing courtesy and assistance in searching out material which I required, and to Professor S. J. Langley of the College of Arts and Science, Baghdad, who has read the proofs and made many valuable suggestions. I am, however, alone responsible for the opinions expressed and for any errors of fact which there may be. I should perhaps add, as my work during recent years has been connected with government departments, that the views expressed in this book do not necessarily in any way reflect the views of those government departments to which I have been attached.

K. G. FENELON

Baghdad, Iraq.

Contents

Contents

Illustrations

CHAPTER ONE

Retrospect

Time which changes all things, has gradually changed the circumstances of this Kingdom.[1]

MOST countries produce the bulk of their own food. Only a very few, notably Britain, Belgium, Holland, Switzerland and Norway, import more than a third of their total food supply and among these Britain is outstanding as by far the largest buyer, taking before the Second World War no less than 40 per cent of the world's total trade in food and animal feedingstuffs. Though one of the two most densely populated industrial countries in the world, Britain was also one of the best-fed nations in the world, having an exceptionally varied and attractive diet, in which not much more than a third of the total energy value was obtained from bulky, starchy foods such as cereals and potatoes. It was only in the United States, Australia, New Zealand and Denmark, that the diet showed a lower proportionate consumption of these less attractive foods and then but very slightly less.

Historically, the phenomenon of a Britain, densely populated per square mile of area and relying on imports for about two-thirds of her food, is of comparatively recent emergence. In the space of about two hundred years, Britain's population increased about eight-fold and food imports grew from the merest trickle to something like five million tons of wheat and flour, a somewhat similar tonnage of maize and other animal feedingstuffs, two million tons of sugar, nearly one-and-a-half million tons of meat and some two-and-a-half million tons of fruit and vegetables.

Looking back over the centuries, it is surprising to find how

[1] David Davies. *The case of Labourers in Husbandry Stated and Considered*, 1795.

limited in number were the foods consumed by the ordinary person in this country. Many foods now popular and in general favour among all classes are historically of recent introduction. This is especially true of vegetables. The development of transport and world communications together with the introduction of refrigeration and cold storage has added immensely to the variety of foods in the diets of the ordinary person. In the past, the winter months were the testing time for food supplies as food could not be preserved to any extent, and even cattle had to be killed off as the pastures were incapable of carrying them over the winter. To-day, thanks to world supplies and refrigeration, even the lowest-paid workers in the towns can have a greater variety of winter foods than any but the richest could in the past.

In comparison with Continental countries, Britain fed well, and was for centuries noted for her solid fare—the roast beef of Old England has passed into a legend. Special attention was paid by the legislature and the local authorities to maintain the standards as is attested for example by the Assizes of Bread and Ale. London in particular was proud of her reputation for good food and drink. Each year by ancient custom the Lord Mayor accompanied by the ale conners visited the taverns, and if the quality were up to standard, a garland was hung out. The ceremony has been recorded in popular verse as follows:

"Landlord, bring out your brew of ale;
We want no tipple thin or stale!"

The conners tasted, smacked their lips, then proclaimed:

"Good, sir, 'tis faultless, we declare
Please hang the garland, my Lord Mayor."

After the ceremony, the Lord Mayor with other guests partook of the landlord's hospitality, which would include a wassail bowl, lamb's wool,[1] fettled porter and mulled ale.

[1] Hot spiced ale mixed with the pulp of roasted apples.

The eighteenth century was a turning point in the history of Britain's food supplies, for the year 1750 marked the approximate beginning of a vast upswing in population growth. At Domesday the population of England and Wales was probably about one-and-a-half millions. About 1500 it may have been three millions, having perhaps doubled in the four preceding centuries. During the first half of the eighteenth century, it reached six millions, having taken about 250 years to double itself. It doubled again, however, in little more than seventy years, being twelve millions in 1821. The next doubling took place in less than sixty years, but after that the rate of increase slowed down somewhat. For Scotland, reliable estimates relating to population are not available for the earlier years, but after 1821 population doubled in a little over seventy years; after that the rate of growth was rather less than in England and Wales.[1]

Food in the Eighteenth Century. To understand Britain's food problems of to-day and to see the position in its proper perspective some account of the main dietary changes and of the development of British agriculture is necessary, though it is not proposed to go back further than the eighteenth century.[2]

In the first half of that century, all the main staple foods were plentiful and cheap, though there was not, of course, anything like the variety to which we have become accustomed to-day. Among all classes, except the smaller tenant farmers who had suffered a setback owing to the growth of larger estates, there was a marked improvement in standards of living as compared with the previous century. There were very few years of droughts, bad harvests or wet summers, and though wages remained at much the same rate as they had been for many years previously, the cost of living fell as a result of the plentiful supply of all the main foods. Wages of labourers

---

[1] See Statistical Appendix, Table 1.

[2] Those interested in the history of Britain's food will find much useful information in Drummond and Wilbraham, *The Englishman's Food*, N. Curtis-Bennett, *The Food of the People*, and W. Ashley, *The Bread of Our Forefathers*.

and the less skilled workmen ranged from 7s. to 9s. a week, much as they had been for nearly a century, but food fell in price, meat for example falling in price from 5d. or 6d. a pound to 2d. or 3d. There was plenty of work to be had both on the land and in the new towns. Improvement in conditions of living was particularly marked in the case of the agricultural labourers as they were assured of work, and food was so cheap that they could afford meat several times a week. They also had gardens in which they could cultivate a variety of vegetables unknown to their fathers or grandfathers. The staple diet in the South was bread, butter and cheese with meat appearing on the table as stated above perhaps two or three times a week. Cabbages, carrots, onions and other vegetables from the garden provided the materials for soups and savoury stews. In the North, less meat was eaten, but there was more milk and the potato was rapidly becoming a usual garden crop.

In the second half of the century, however, things changed for the worse and by the end of the century, the condition of the rural labourers in the South had deteriorated so greatly that they were living almost exclusively on bread. In the North, the variety of food remained much greater. During the second part of the century, the rapid growth of population made heavy demands on the production of wheat, and a disastrous sequence of wet seasons and bad harvests from 1764 to 1775 led to high prices for foodstuffs. In 1765, there was a grave dearth and in 1776 the quartern loaf reached the unprecedented price of 1s. 6d. Though the duty on imported corn was suspended, this did not help very much because there was a bad harvest on the Continent. When the century closed, a large proportion of the population was facing dearth, depression and distress. This was the sombre background against which Thomas Malthus published his First Essay on Population. Malthus did not, and indeed could not, then foresee the immense supplies of foodstuffs which were to come from the New World as a result of the revolution in transport which was effected after 1870.

Much valuable information on the amount and kind of

food eaten at the close of the eighteenth century by the agricultural labourers, then a relatively much larger sector of the population than now, is available to us from family budgets, probably the earliest of their kind, collected and published by the Reverend David Davies,[1] Rector of Barkham, in Berkshire, and by Sir Frederic Eden.[2]

The humane and kindly Rector of Barkham, who collected budgets of the earnings and expenses of labouring families in his Parish at about Easter 1787, refers in the preface to his book to the "real, widespread and increasing distress" among agricultural labourers. As a result of the interest aroused by the distribution of these budgets among various correspondents, he was able to add budgets from twenty-seven other parishes distributed among seventeen counties as well as some budgets from Scotland which latter he found to furnish "wonderful instances of good economy."

It may be of interest to reproduce some of these budgets as they are probably the earliest examples of a method which is now in universal use in connection with studies in nutrition, poverty, wage questions and other sociological investigations. One cannot of course generalize from a few instances, but the budgets are sufficiently typical for families with young children; and there was then greater uniformity in the kinds of food consumed in the different districts (though not necessarily in the dishes prepared with these foods) except for the marked difference between North and South England. Overleaf is one of the budgets from Barkham set out in full for a family of seven persons.

Davies found that among the families in Barkham which he investigated, few could afford more than one pound of meat weekly. The amount of tea consumed per family was about one to one-and-a-half ounces a week at 2d. an ounce. For soft sugar, it was half-a-pound at 7d. to 8d. a pound, salt-butter or lard half-a-pound at 7½d. to 8d. a pound. Malt was so dear that they seldom brewed any small beer though Davies

---

[1] *The Case of Labourers in Husbandry Stated and Considered*, 1795.
[2] *The State of the Poor*, 1797.

A Household Budget of 1787

Expenses per week	£	s.	d.	Earnings per week	£	s.	d.
Flour. 7½ gal.		6	3	The man earns at a			
Yeast for bread-making			2½	medium		8	0
Salt			1½	The woman			6
Bacon 1 lb.			8	The children			0
Tea 1 oz.			2				
Sugar ¾ lb.			6				
Butter ½ lb.			4				
Cheese (seldom any)			0				
Beer (seldom any)			0				
Soap ¼ lb. starch, blue			2¼				
Candles ⅛ lb.			3				
Thread, thrum, worsted			3				
Total		8	11¼	Total		8	6

	£	s.	d.		£	s.	d.
Amount per annum	£23	4	9	Amount per annum	£22	2	0

	£	s.	d.
Rent, fuel, clothes, lying-in, etc.	£6	0	0
Total of expenses per annum	£29	4	9
Total of earnings per annum	£22	2	0
Deficiency of earnings	£7	2	9

The family consisted of a man, his wife and five children, the eldest eight years of age, the youngest an infant. The deficiency in earnings would have to be made good by resort to the Poor Law, and Davies estimated that the number of persons assisted by the Poor Law in his Parish was about one-fifth of the whole, apart from those assisted occasionally in sickness.

maintained "surely it is reasonable" that they should be enabled to brew small beer for themselves.

Davies also published many budgets which he had collected from his correspondents and it may be of interest by way of illustrating the variations in diet and the differences of standdards, as between North and South, to summarize some of the budgets, including that of the Barkham family previously quoted.

Expenses per week on Food.	Barkham, Berkshire 1787 7 persons		Tanfield, Co. Durham 1789 7 persons		Gt. Eccleston, Lancashire 1789 7 persons		Marton, Westmoreland 1790 7 persons	
	s.	d.	s.	d.	s.	d.	s.	d.
Bread and flour— wheaten	6	3	1	0				
Bread and flour— other			2	0	3	0	4	6
Oatmeal				4				
Milk			1	2		5½	1	2
Potatoes				4		6	1	3
Meat or bacon		8		8		4		
Tea, sugar, butter	1	0		8	1	2	1	2
Cheese				5				
Salt		1½		1		1½		1
Yeast		2½						
Total expenditure on food	8	3	6	8	5	7	8	2

Notes. Expenditure on salt by the Tanfield family is estimated from an item including soap, salt and candles. In the Lancashire family treacle was included with the item tea, sugar and butter and the item for milk included some beer.

The main differences in the Northern and Southern diets lay in the preference for white bread in the South whereas in the North rye or barley bread and oatmeal were consumed instead. Many contemporaries argued that the distress of the poor in the South was due to their own lack of frugality and their indulgence in the extravagance of wheaten bread, whereas formerly they ate bread of a cheaper variety. They were also blamed for neglecting the use of potatoes, and for drinking excessive quantities of tea. Pitt among others referred to the "groundless prejudices" against mixed bread of barley, rye and wheat, but all attempts to popularize substitutes for white bread in the South failed. There were, however, some sound grounds for these prejudices which were fully explained by

Davies. In the North and in other countries, the people, though eating bread made of rye, barley or oats, had milk, cheese, butter, fruits and fish to eat with their coarser bread. This, he pointed out, was formerly the case in the South of England when meat, butter and cheese were sufficiently cheap that poor people could well afford their use. Oatmeal eaten with milk is a very different food from oatmeal eaten by itself and it was not for choice but of necessity that the Southern labourers went without milk. After the spread of agricultural enclosures, the labourers could no longer keep a cow, and the milk produced by the large farmers went to the towns. This scarcity of milk and the high price of malt probably encouraged the spread of tea-drinking among the poor. Tea, being a mild stimulant, was also attractive to persons whose food was monotonous and insipid. It is evident from the family budgets collected by Davies and Eden that tea was in general use among poor families by the end of the eighteenth century. The tea drunk by the poor was, however, very different from that sipped by the fashionable tea-drinkers of London, being in the words of Davies, "spring water just coloured with a few leaves of the lowest-priced tea and sweetened with the brownest sugar". "Tea drinking," he said, "is not the cause but the consequence of the distress of the poor."

Both Davies and Eden refer to the effects of a fuel shortage on food habits. The high price of fuel in the South encouraged labourers to buy wheaten bread from the bakers rather than bake for themselves as was usual in the North, where indeed home baking has continued down to the present day. In the South, it was also the custom, when a family had any meat, to get it cooked at the local bakery.

Sir Frederic Eden, who made a thorough study of family budgets up and down the country, was able to show that in the North of England, Scotland and Wales, the poorest labourers regaled themselves with a variety of dishes unknown in the South. Among these he frequently mentions *hasty pudding* made of oatmeal, water and salt which was eaten with a little milk or beer poured upon it, with treacle or with a little cold butter put in the middle. Another favourite dish was *crowdie,* common among miners in the North, and made with boiling water and oatmeal and eaten with milk or butter. *Frumenty* or barley milk as made in the North consisted of barley with the husks off, boiled in water for nearly two hours and mixed with skimmed milk. The principal advantage, according to Eden, which the labourers of the North of England possessed over those in the South consisted in the great variety of cheap and savoury soups which the use of barley and barley bread afforded them the opportunity of making. He also saw in the cheapness of fuel another reason why the meals of the Northern labourer were so much more diversified and his table so often supplied with hot dishes. To the present day, these traditions have to some extent persisted, and the North rightly prides itself on its own special dishes and good fare.

Food Growing in the Eighteenth Century. The rapid growth of population in the eighteenth century, the development of manufacturing industry and the expansion of the towns greatly increased the market for food and especially that for wheat and meat. Farmers as a result of this increasing demand found it paid them to increase the acreage under wheat and also to increase the size of their herds and flocks. When prices rose after 1750, there was an even greater inducement to adopt more intensive methods of farming. Land which had escaped enclosure in previous centuries was rapidly fenced in and con-solidated into large fields. In the process much waste and common land which had served to provide grazing facilities for the small farmers and labourers was brought into the new farms. Improvements in arable farming necessitated this process of enclosure, and there is no doubt but that standards of farming were vastly improved, especially in the second half of the century, and it has therefore with reason been called the "agricultural revolution". The great landowners and the large farmers prospered as a result of the adoption of new methods and the evolution of improved strains of livestock. The small holders and the agricultural labourers on the other hand suffered greatly, especially from the loss of their rights to use the commons and waste lands. Improved agricultural methods also meant that less labour was required per acre, though more food was produced, and in consequence many villages were depopulated. The displaced labourers flocked into the towns or migrated to the new industrial areas, where they were gradually absorbed by the factories which were springing up during the industrial revolution. Though the enclosure movement was accompanied by much distress among the agricultural labourers and small holders, it was the essential pre-requisite to improved systems of farming, and it ultimately led to a great expansion in agricultural output.

The Growth of Markets. The increase in population, the growth of towns and the transformation of agriculture from predominatingly subsistence farming to farming for the market led to the development of a highly-organized system of distribution. The food markets of London and the larger towns began to attract produce from far afield. Transport, until the railways were built in the following century, presented great difficulties, yet despite these difficulties choice foods were dispatched to the London markets from surprisingly distant parts of the Kingdom. Fresh salmon for example was carried by relays of horsemen travelling as fast as man and beast could go from Berwick-on-Tweed, while great droves of cattle, herds of pigs and flocks of sheep, geese and turkeys moved on their own feet along the soft, less-used by-ways. Highland cattle tramped from Scotland to the Norfolk meadows, there to be fattened and marched off in weekly droves to the markets of London. From the summer and autumn fairs of Wales, great herds of Welsh cattle travelled to South-east England. Even the geese and turkeys of Norfolk were driven on foot to the metropolis, the turkeys being protected from the hard roads by being shod in leather boots, while the geese, which would not allow themselves to be shod, had their feet covered with a coating of tar and grit.

The supply of milk was quite inadequate in the towns despite the fact that the new farming methods had greatly increased milk production in the country districts. Much of this milk which could not be transported over any great distance owing to the deplorably bad state of the highways was converted into butter and cheese, which commodities could be more readily sent by road. As a result, the townsman and more particularly the Londoner came during the eighteenth century to know the many varied types of cheese produced in different parts of the island. Cheddar, Wiltshire, Stilton, Gloucester and Double Gloucester and many other cheeses by the end of the century had achieved a national repute, whereas a generation or two before they were practically unknown outside their own local area.

During the century there was also a rapid expansion in market gardening, particularly in the vicinity of London. The orchards of Kent rapidly expanded during this century.

In short, the food markets of London were attracting produce of all kinds. Fruit, vegetables, meat, poultry, game, shell fish, spices, oranges and lemons, indeed practically every form of food in its almost infinite variety was coming to converge on London from home and overseas.

On the tables of the well-to-do, the abundance and quality of the foods served at a dinner party of those days is almost staggering to us of a less leisured generation, and one which has been nurtured on war and post-war austerities. A detailed account of a dinner party of those days will serve better, perhaps, to indicate the kind and variety of food which was then frequently provided for the guests than would a long list of the commodities available in the shops and markets. When Parson Woodforde and his wife were invited out to dine on 9 May 1782, he records the event in his Diary as follows:

"We spent a very agreeable and merry Day there. We had for dinner 1st. Course—Stewed Tence, Ham and Fowls, Harrico of Mutton, Peas, Soup, and a Rump of Beef boiled on the side table with roots etc. 2nd Course—Pigeons and Asparagus, Orange Pudding, Maccaroni, Custard, Tarts, and Jelly prettily set of with Blamange coloured like what it represented. Desert—9 dishes—Oranges, Almonds and Raisins, Cherries preserved, Olives, Cakes. Plates and dishes for the desert quite new and very beautiful—Madeira,

Port and Mountain Wines—Parmesan Cheese also at Dinner. After Tea and Coffee we all played at Loo—at which I neither won or lost anything—Nancy lost 6 pence."[1]

Probably the most striking change during the eighteenth century in Britain's food habits was that which has already been referred to, namely the increase in tea drinking by all classes of the community. Tea had fallen considerably in price by the end of the previous century and its consumption expanded enormously after 1700. With the increase in tea drinking, there also went a steady increase in the consumption of sugar, which increase continued apart from a setback during the First World War right up to the Second World War, since when rationing served to curtail consumption.

Exports and Imports. A fortunate succession of good harvests from 1715 to 1764 provided British farmers with a substantial surplus of produce for export abroad which was encouraged by the government by the payment of bounties when the price of corn was low at home. Imports on the other hand were practically prohibited by the heavy duties imposed. During the Napoleonic wars, foreign competition was eliminated and the high prices for corn ruling during this period enabled even poor lands to be cultivated with substantial profits. On the restoration of peace in 1815, however, the artificial boom in agriculture came to a sudden end. Prices of agricultural produce fell, land went out of cultivation and rents dropped. The depression in agriculture lasted for twenty years, and during these years there was no money for improvements and many farm buildings became neglected or even derelict where marginal lands were concerned.

By the time Queen Victoria ascended the throne, the worst of the crisis was over. Rents had been adjusted, the burden of taxes, rates and tithes was reduced and the rapid growth of industry relieved the glut on the agricultural labour market and created an increasing demand for agricultural produce.

[1] *Diary of a Country Parson.* Quoted by G. Reynolds. *Gastronomic Pleasures,* 1950.

With renewed prosperity, agricultural improvements were continued and science came to the help of the farmers. Drainage was effected on an extensive scale, artificial fertilizers came into general use, seed strains were improved, cattle breeding became more scientific and herd books were introduced. Improvements in internal transport enabled the farmers' produce to be marketed over greater distances, and also assisted in the spread of knowledge regarding up-to-date farming methods.

When the Corn Laws were repealed in 1846 as a result of the Irish Famine, there were many who regarded this as a death blow to British agriculture, but in actual fact Britain's adoption of a Free Trade policy did not lead all at once to large-scale imports. For many years, the high cost of transport from the New World acted as an effective protective tariff to British farmers. Other fortuitous circumstances helped to prolong the period of prosperity; the Crimea War closed the Baltic and cut off supplies from Russia, the American Civil War delayed competition from America and the Franco-German War for a time eliminated grain imports from Germany and created a market for British corn in France.

In the eighteen-seventies the position of the British farmer was completely transformed as a result of the great improvement in sea transport brought about by the adoption of the compound steam engine and the opening up of the continental interiors of Canada and the United States by the railroads. British farmers began to feel the full blast of competition from the low cost prairie producers, and they were forced to reorganize their farms and in particular to turn over from arable to meat and dairy products. There was also an increase in market gardening and fruit growing. The transition, however, was slow and the great agricultural depression of the last quarter of the nineteenth century was severely felt by the farmers.

The Urban Consumer. During the nineteenth century, the urban consumer became more and more important as population grew and the towns expanded. His diet gradually but steadily improved. It became richer and more varied and at the same time came to absorb a relatively smaller proportion of his wages. Thus in the first half of the nineteenth century, there was a marked increase in the consumption of butcher's meat which J. R. McCulloch estimated as being twice as great in the London of 1837 as it was in that of 1750. The increase was even greater in certain other parts of the country, and by 1840 the weekly expenditure of factory workers on meat in the industrial towns was nearly equal to that on bread. Consumption of bread, however, was high as compared with present-day standards, being then probably something like 364 lb. a head per annum. By 1881, it had fallen to something like 283 lb. and in 1934 to 198 lb. Consumption of sugar was about 20 lb. a head per annum in the early years of the century, but a hundred years later it was five times as great. Milk consumption did not increase appreciably; one reason being that milk had about doubled in price whereas sugar had halved, and bread and flour had remained about the same. This is a striking illustration of the advantages which the industrialized, urban classes owed to cheap imported food. Milk had to be home-produced while sugar and flour could be imported.

These changes in the types of food demanded were made possible by the fact that the growth of population, great as it was, was accompanied by an even faster growth in the national income. After the turn of the century the continued increase in real incomes per head led to increased consumption of the relatively more expensive foods such as meat, butter, milk, fruit and vegetables. The abnormal conditions of the 1914–18 war halted this progress and turned the nation back to a diet in which cereals bulked larger, and in which meat, fats, eggs and tea showed a reduced consumption. There was a considerable reduction in the consumption of sugar. According to the Report of the Committee on the Increase in the Cost of Living to the Working Classes (Cd. 8980) the change in the nutritive value of the diet, however, was not very great. After the Armistice the movement towards a more varied diet began again, and continued at an increasing rate. Between 1909 and 1936, for example, fruit consumption increased by 88 per cent, vegetables (other than potatoes) by 64 per cent and butter and eggs by about 50 per cent. The demand for bread on a *per capita* basis dropped to nearly half what it had been a century before.[1]

Statistical Investigations. For the first part of the nineteenth century there is little statistical information available relating to family food consumption. The pioneer in the detailed study of family income and expenditure was Le Play, who in his classic work on the subject entitled *Les Ouvriers Européens*, published in 1855, included four typical budgets from England, covering London, Sheffield and Derbyshire. These budgets are for the families of industrial workers, cutlers, foundrymen and carpenters, and they reveal that the town workers had a wide variety of foods which they could afford to buy, markedly contrasting in variety and palatability with the limited diets of the century before. Wheaten bread, husked barley, oats and rice figured in the budgets with butter, lard, cheese, fresh milk, eggs and potatoes. The meats consumed comprised beef, lamb, veal and pork, and a Christmas goose. There was a wide range of vegetables bought at various seasons of the year, including cauliflowers, garden beans, green peas, carrots, onions, cucumbers, salads, turnips, lettuce, cress and celery. Gooseberries, apples, cherries, plums, pears and currants were included among the fruits. As might be expected, tea, sugar and treacle figured prominently in the purchases.

The next important investigation which merits consideration was concerned with the health aspects of the food problem and is of special interest in that it attempted to set up standards for the food requirements of the individual and to determine the cost of purchasing a sufficient amount of food. In 1858, the Privy Council, then the central medical authority for the country, at the instigation of its chief medical officer, J. Simon, began to interest itself in "the circumstances which regulate the distribution of disease in England". In setting on foot an inquiry into this question, it included an investigation into the sufficiency of the food available to the poorest classes of the population. When the Cotton Famine of 1862, brought about by the American Civil War, led to severe and

[1] E. M. H. Lloyd. *Food Supplies and Consumption at Different Income Levels.* Journal of Agricultural Economics Society, 1936. Vol. IV.

prolonged unemployment among the cotton operatives of Lancashire and other centres of the industry, it requested Dr. E. Smith, a physician who had interested himself in studies of nutrition; to undertake a special inquiry into standards for measuring dietary requirements and the minimum cost of purchasing food sufficient to avert starvation diseases from the unemployed population. Smith was also asked to determine what would be the most useful expenditure, with special reference to health, of a weekly minimum allowance granted exclusively for the purchase of food and how any small additional sums might be most usefully expended.

Smith's standards were expressed, not as we would express them to-day in terms of calories, proteins and other nutrients, but in terms of grains of carbon and nitrogen. These standards were then translated into fifty diet sheets, setting out the foods to be eaten on a daily or weekly basis, for the cotton operatives to follow or for use in emergency canteens. It would seem that Smith's standards enjoyed a considerable vogue and were used to assess the value of the diets of agricultural and industrial workers during the subsequent decade. A popular version of the report was published as a *Practical Dietary for the use of Schools, Families and Labouring Classes.*

The first modern statistical investigation into expenditure on various foodstuffs and estimates of consumption *per capita* was undertaken in 1881 by a Committee of the British Association for the Advancement of Science.[1] This Committee was required by its terms of reference to consider "The present appropriation of wages and other sources of income and how far it is consonant with the economic progress of the people of the United Kingdom".

In its report, the Committee showed that in 1880 the largest item of expenditure on food was for meat, and the next largest bread, closely followed by beer. The main items of food expenditure averaged over the whole population and as calculated by the Committee are set out in the following table.

---

[1] *Reports of the British Association,* 1881 (pp. 272–89) and 1882 (pp. 297–306).

Expenditure per head per day, 1880

	d.		d.
Meat	1·87	Potatoes	0·64
Bread	1·41	Tea	0·60
Beer	1·40	Fruit and vegetables	0·51
Milk and eggs	0·78	Sugar	0·50
Butter and cheese	0·67		

The Committee also investigated the consumption of imported foods, and found that this had greatly increased between 1840 and 1880. The figures which were calculated on a *per capita* basis strikingly emphasize the growing importance of imported foods in this period as will be seen from the table below.

Imported food retained for home consumption in lb. per head of the population, United Kingdom

	1840 lb.	1860 lb.	1880 lb.
Corn	42·5	118·9	210·0
Bacon and ham	—	1·3	16·0
Butter	1·1	3·3	7·4
Cheese	0·9	2·2	5·6
Sugar	15·2	33·1	63·7
Tea	1·2	2·7	4·6
Eggs (number)	3·6	5·8	21·7

Commenting on the trend of these figures, the report stated: "A large consumption of articles of food in great part imported is a sign of general prosperity, and is conducive of greater effectiveness of labour. There is no reason to suppose that home production has diminished of late years except indeed as the consequence of deficient harvest on special years."

Using the data provided by the report to compare 1938 with 1880, it will be found that the consumption of meat increased by 45 per cent over 1880, that of sugar by 40 per cent, and that of tea[1] and butter by 100 per cent. On the other

[1] C. H. Denyer pointed out in an article in the Economic Journal of March, 1893, that the consumption of tea was rising steadily. In 1852 it was 1·99 lb. a head per annum but by 1891 it had risen to 5·35 lb.

hand, the consumption of bread and potatoes was 30 per cent less in 1938 than it was in 1880.

Towards the end of the century, family budgets were collected and published by the Economic Club[1] and other organizations, while in 1904 the Board of Trade undertook a large scale collection of working-class budgets to form a basis for the Cost of Living Index Number which remained as the main official source of information on this subject until 1947, when it was superseded by the Interim Index of Retail Prices. The results of the 1904 investigation were published in a White Paper with the unrevealing title, *A Memorandum on British and Foreign Trade and Industry* (Cd. 2337) and the information then collected was supplemented in 1912 by a further inquiry into working-class rents and retail prices. (Cd. 6955).

---

[1] *Family Budgets, being the income and expenses of twenty-eight British Households, 1891–94.*

CHAPTER TWO

Diversity of Foods

National and Regional Differences in Diet. The term food covers a multitude of commodities. Though one man's food may not exactly be another man's poison, there are great differences both quantitatively and qualitatively in the food and dietary habits of different peoples. Popular tradition for example associates roast beef with Old England, oatmeal with Scotland, potatoes with Ireland, macaroni with Italy and sausages with Germany. A list of foods special to, or closely associated with particular countries, could be almost indefinitely extended from the kedgeree of India to the grenouilles or escargots of France. In almost every country, there is to be found some typical food which has attained an important position in the diet of the particular nation either through choice or from necessity. Necessity here as elsewhere may be the mother of invention. The goulashes and similar traditional dishes of Continental Europe probably had their origin in the need of making the best use of the poorer quality joints and of making the meat go further; much less meat having been consumed per head in most European countries before the war than in Great Britain.

National diets are determined by many factors among which incomes, natural resources, tradition and habit are important. For the world as a whole, income is the most significant factor in determining a nation's diet. In general, prosperous nations fare well nutritionally, poor countries fare badly, and the richer the nation the more varied the diet. The poorer nations in general consume a higher proportion of cereals or potatoes which are rich in the energy-giving carbohydrates but make for a monotonous diet. In countries such as Java, Indo-China, Yugoslavia or Japan, over three-quarters of the total calories in the diet are derived from cereals and tubers. In comparison, the proportion of cereals and starchy foods in the diets of the United States, Australia and New Zealand is less than a third.

Rice, wheat and maize are the three main cereal foods of the world and of these rice is quantitatively the most important as it is the staple food of more than half the human race. Rice provides a high calorie yield per acre and therefore is grown where possible in preference to other crops where the amount of arable land available per head of the population is small.

Natural resources and climate may greatly influence the food of a people. Thus the inhabitants of Argentina, Uruguay and Paraguay are great meat-eaters whereas those of Iceland eat little meat but much fish. The environmental factor in diet is often significant and serves to explain what are often regarded as the peculiar dishes of certain countries such as bamboo shoots in China, the sea-weed foods of Japan, or the "edible earths" of Africa.[1]

Readers of Hilaire Belloc will probably recall in connection with the diversity of human foods his description of the queer dishes eaten in certain countries, and his mock lamentation:

> "Alas! what various tastes in food
> Divide the human brotherhood."

Tradition and habit are of considerable influence in determining national diets. Nations are often very conservative in their food habits and tend to resent any changes in what have become their traditional foods. This may be unreasonable and the result of prejudice alone but not infrequently there may be good reasons behind the resistance to change, tradition having rightly determined a suitable diet for their special needs. "No matter how unusual a traditional diet may appear, it ought never to be condemned until its nutritional composition is known. It is upon this basis alone that nutritional adequacy can be assessed."[2] Sometimes, however,

---

[1] See W. Godden. Notes of certain edible earths and native salts from Nigeria. *West African Medical Journal*, 1929. Vol. 2.

[2] Magnus Pyke. *Industrial Nutrition*, page 3.

food prejudices have grown up which are hard to explain on any rational grounds such as for example the superstitions against the eating of blackberries in certain countries where they grow wild in ample profusion, and would provide an attractive addition to the diet. To take another example, in Britain only one or two varieties of wild mushrooms are regarded with favour whereas in France there is a great profusion in the varieties collected for the table. Wild fruits and plants nowadays are often left ungathered, though formerly prized and of great nutritive value. Fruits such as elderberries and hips and haws, plants such as nettles, lady smock, corn salad, fennel, sorrel and dandelions, or seaweeds such as laver, can make valuable additions to the larder.[1] Many of the fruits are suitable for preserving and in this way could supply variety to meals in the winter months when fresh fruit is difficult to obtain.

In Europe, each nation has developed its own traditional pattern of food consumption, France in particular being renowned for a highly civilized attitude to food and wine. This interest in food permeates all classes in France and each of the Provinces has tended to develop its own regional specialities.

The French gourmet prizes many foods little known in other countries and in particular shows a great partiality for the "fruits of the sea" including oursins (sea-urchins), claires, belons and marennes.

Regional differences which give such a distinctive character to the French cuisine, are also to be found in other countries including our own. In the previous chapter, reference was made to the marked differences between the diets of Southern and Northern England but a further and more detailed examination would show that every county has its own specialities.[2] In the past when the means of communication were undeveloped, there was an even greater variety of dishes special to particular parts of the country. Some of these have now disappeared but many of them have been preserved in

[1] See Jason Hill. *Wild Foods of Britain*, 1941.
[2] See *Receipts and Relishes being a* vade-mecum *for the Epicure in the British Isles*.

the kitchens of the farm-houses and cottages. Among the great profusion of county specialities, there may be instanced the lardy cakes of Wiltshire, the singing hinnies of Durham, so-called because being so rich, they sing or sizzle while they cook, Lincolnshire haslet, Buckinghamshire pie, Devonshire splits, Yorkshire Pudding, Lancashire hot-pot, Darlington's Granny Loaf, Cornish pasties, the cowheel pie of Lancashire, and the rum butter of Cumberland. The Severn Valley has its potted lampreys, Shropshire its figet pie, Tyneside its pan-haggledy[1] and Edinburgh its "petticoat tails".[2] With cakes, the local varieties are legion: Banbury Cakes, Eccles Cakes, Gosnargh Cakes, Bath Buns, Pontefract Cakes, Abingdon Critten Cakes, Kentish Huffkins, the Sally Lunn's of Bath, the Black Cakes of North Devon, Crempog of Wales, Chelsea Buns, Bakewell Tart, Yorkshire Cheese Cakes and in Scotland, Montrose Cakes, Parlies and Ayrshire Shortcakes.

Many towns boast of their gingerbread including Market Drayton, Grantham, Ormskirk, Congleton, Wrexham and Fochabers. There are also the Gingerbread Husbands of Gloucestershire, the Gingerbread Valentines of Bath, Wide-combe Fair's Spiced Ale and Gingerbread and the Parliament Cakes of London.

Local specialities often rejoice in strange or fascinating names such as the "Thunder and Lightning" of Cornwall (Cornish splits eaten with cream and treacle or jam); "Star-Gazy Pie" (Cornish fish pie made with the heads of the fishes sticking out of the pastry and with parsley placed in their mouths); "Huckle-my-Buff", (Sussex colloquial name for egg-flip to which beer has been added); "Love in Disguise" (Herefordshire calf's heart dish); "Hough and Dough" (Northamptonshire boiled suet pudding); "Fat Rascals" (Yorkshire currant biscuits); "Haggamuggi" (a Shetland fish liver dish) or "Stanhope Firelighters" (a Durham cake made from oats, butter and sugar in equal weights).

Scotland has numerous national dishes of its own, some of

[1] A dish of strips of bacon fried with sliced potatoes and onions.
[2] A kind of shortbread in small triangular cakes, said by some to have derived its name from *petit gâteaux* during the days of the "Auld Alliance".

which like haggis, oatcakes, shortbread, Scotch Broth and mealie puddings have a world-wide reputation. Among many others, less well-known perhaps outside Scotland, are Bannocks (large scones), Baps (breakfast rolls), Bawd Bree (Scots Hare Soup), Cockie Leekie (boiled fowl, scraggy beef, leeks and prunes), Gundy (brown sugar, butter and treacle boiled until thick and a with little aniseed or cinnamon added), Kail Brose (cabbage broth), and Tatties and Herrin'.

Sometimes the traditional dishes of a county may take many forms. Thus the Cornish Pasty varies according to the filling though the method of making it does not differ, there being for example Meat and Potato Pasty, Rabbity Pasty, Eggy Pasty and Apple Pasty.

Some dishes by long tradition are associated with certain festivals or seasons of the year, and these range from our Christmas turkeys and pudding, Shrove Tuesday pancakes or our Easter Eggs to Hot Cross Buns, the Michaelmas Goose, the Simnel Cakes of Mothering Sunday and the Hallow E'en Apples or to special local customs such as those of Fenstanton where frumenty was eaten on the First of May or of Hampshire where wafers are eaten on Mothering Sunday. Other examples are the Dumb Cakes made and eaten on Christmas Eve and St. Mark's Eve in Northamptonshire, Wilfra Tarts eaten during the first week of August in Ripon to commemorate the re-entry of St. Wilfred into the town, and Plum Shuttles in Rutland, so-called because the bun is of an oval shape like a weaver's shuttle, eaten on St. Valentine's Day. Certain trades also have been accustomed to celebrate the Feast Day of their Patron Saint with special dishes such as the Cattern Cakes made by Bedfordshire lacemakers on St. Catherine's Day (25 November). In the early morning of that day in some of the lace-making towns or villages a bellman went round crying:

"Rise, Maids, rise!
Bake your Cattern pies
Bake enough and bake no waste
And let the Bellman have a taste."[1]

[1] Quoted in *Traditional Fare of England and Wales*, compiled by the

3

Tandra Cakes were made by Pavenham Lacemakers on St. Andrew's Day (30 November) which was celebrated instead of "Catterns" in certain districts. Snails, which are eaten in Northumberland from spring to autumn, used to be the traditional fare at the Glassmakers' feast.

When times were hard, necessity led to the introduction of frugal dishes, some of which survived when conditions improved. "Bolton Brewis" for example dates from the "Hungry Forties" and in its simplest form, it is made by pouring boiling water over a crust of bread. The water is then drained off and pepper and salt are sprinkled on the bread. In more prosperous times, Brewis is made with water in which pork has been boiled, oatcakes are used instead of bread crusts, and the dish is eaten with black puddings. Another "hard times dish" known as "Cold Water Willies" was to be found in Northumberland, being made from flour and salt with just enough water added to make a pliable dough. They were also nicknamed "Tough Cake and Pull-it," as they were so hard that they had to be pulled to pieces before eating.

To some extent food preparation has been influenced by local variations in the kind and availability of fuel and in the types of ovens and kitchen utensils traditional in different districts. Tradition, springing initially no doubt from some circumstance peculiar to the district such as local supplies of particular ingredients or peculiarities in the type of kitchen equipment, has also influenced the way in which a particular food or dish is prepared. Thus the apple pie of Hereford is not the same as that of Somerset and dumplings may vary greatly from one part of the country to another. Flead cakes in Cheshire, Wiltshire and Sussex are very different from each other.

The influence of environmental conditions on diet is well illustrated by the prevalence of fish-liver dishes in the Shetlands, including such specialities as Krampus (Sillock livers melted in fat and with oatmeal added), Kroppen (steamed fish liver, meal and a fish head stuffed with herbs), Liver Flakki

National Federation of Women's Institutes. This book contains many traditional recipes collected by members of the Institutes.

(fish and fish livers) or Liver-Krus (fish livers cooked in oat-meal dough, formed into the shape of a cruse or small bowl). In the Orkneys, there are to be found many unusual dishes made from oatmeal including Bere-meal Porridge, Broonie, Burston and Sour Skons. Seaweeds are also eaten in Scotland especially in the Western Islands. These include Sloke Soup in the Hebrides, Dulse in the Isle of Barra and Sea Tangle, which is often eaten raw by children in the Orkneys or roasted in Barra where it is put on buttered barley bannocks.

Certain areas of the country have become noted for the production of choice varieties of food, due often in the first place at any rate to some local advantage of climate, soil or other cause. To cite a few examples, more or less at random, there are Devonshire Cider, Welsh Lamb, Scottish Mutton, Bath Chaps, Whitstable Oysters, Morecambe Shrimps, Wilt-shire Bacon, Aylesbury Ducks, Norfolk Turkeys, Surrey Fowl and York Ham. Among cheeses a great variety is to be found, almost every locality having its own speciality: Cheddar, Cheshire (in three colours—"red", "white" and "blue"), Stilton, Gloucester, Double Gloucester, Cottenham, Slipcote, Derbyshire, Caerphilly, Scottish Dunlop, Blue Veiny (Dorset), Lancashire, Leicestershire, Lincolnshire and Wensleydale. The most popular British cheeses are Cheshire and Cheddar which pre-war accounted in equal shares for 70 per cent of the total factory-produced cheeses in this country. Cheshire led in farm-house production, accounting for over 55 per cent of the total cheese produced, Cheddar followed, being 26 per cent of all farm-house cheeses. Lancashire cheese came next in order of popularity, being about 11 per cent of factory pro-duction and nearly 14 per cent of farm-produced cheeses. Although not very well known outside the County, because being a soft cheese it is difficult to transport, it is in great demand in Lancashire especially in the industrial areas of the South. It is deemed excellent for toasting, when it is often known as "Leigh Toaster". Stilton, accounting pre-war for somewhat over 7 per cent of factory production, is chiefly made in the Melton Mowbray district and is regarded by many connoisseurs as the Queen of British Cheeses. Caerphilly, a mild flavoured cheese, is made for a special market, namely the mining communities of Wales and South-West England. Derbyshire is the oldest of our national cheeses, and in former days each farmhouse had its own method of manufacture; those able to make the better cheeses keeping the method a family secret. Dunlop takes its name from the town of Dunlop in North Ayrshire where it has been made for at least 250 years. Its manufacture is still mainly confined to small farms in South-West Scotland.

The trend nowadays is towards a greater degree of dietary uniformity throughout the country, and in the process, unfortunately, some of the best local traditions of food preparation or usage are in danger of being lost. Home baking, which has long survived in Yorkshire, Durham, Northumberland and the West Country, and local cheese-making are cases in point. War-time shortages, food controls and difficulties of housekeeping have accelerated a process which was well under way in the eighteenth century when William Cobbett thundered against the decay of home brewing. Home bread-making, like home brewing, is now a lost art or practically so, and yet not a hundred years ago J. R. McCulloch[1] could still say: "In many parts of England, it is the custom of private families to bake their own bread. This is particularly the case in Kent and in some parts of Lancashire. In 1801, there was not a single public baker in Manchester; and their number is still very limited."

Food Groups. Food is the prime necessity for growth and existence, but quantity is not the only criterion. Many other factors are involved, some of which have only comparatively recently become known. Food is required not only as a fuel, providing energy and heat when consumed by the body, but also to make good wastage of tissues and to provide for growth in the young. By far the larger proportion of the solid matter in food is used as fuel by the body, though some of it may be stored in the tissues in the form of fat or animal starch (glycogen). If a person is well fed, these stores are constantly replenished and should such a person be deprived of food, he

[1] *Dictionary of Commerce.* New Edition, 1859, p. 194.

can fall back on these resources until they are used up. Thereafter he will become more and more emaciated until death by starvation takes place. Body-building foods cannot be stored in the same way, but have to be provided daily. Lack of them in young persons will stunt growth.

Practically all foodstuffs (other than water) will provide energy and heat, but to maintain the relatively stable structure of the bones, muscles, nerves and internal organs, specialized and often very complex substances must be provided by food. Lime salts in association with phosphorus are required for the hard matter of bones and teeth. For the growth and maintenance of soft tissues such as muscles, complex organic substances called proteins are required. Food also helps to protect the body from disease and so in addition to the energy foods (those containing sugar, starch or fats such as bread, potatoes and margarine) and the body-building foods (those containing protein and mineral salts such as meat, cheese and eggs) there is a third group of protective foods (containing vitamins such as fruit, vegetables and dairy produce).

The body is able to break down foodstuffs by the process of digestion and to synthesize them again into substances which it requires. Some substances, however, it cannot synthesize. Obviously the chemical elements such as calcium, iron or phosphorus are in this group, but so also are a number of complex substances which enter into the composition of human protein and a number of chemical agencies which promote the intricate series of changes from cell to cell. They have all to be obtained directly from food more or less in their original complex state. Among them are the vitamins, which are very diverse both in their chemical constitution and in their functions. They are essential to the health of the body.

However plentiful a diet may be, if it is deficient in one or more nutrients it may be a poor diet. This has led to the idea of a balanced diet—that is a diet balanced in terms of proteins, vitamins and mineral salts—and in the years immediately preceding the Second World War, much was done to popularize the fundamentals of good nutrition by disseminating knowledge of the three-fold needs of the body for energy foods, body-building foods and the "protective foods". During the war with its stresses and food shortages, the Ministry of Food undertook a widespread publicity campaign to spread knowledge of the value of body-building and protective foods. Many attractive posters with arresting slogans were issued among which may be instanced that of an elephant holding a cabbage in its trunk, knotted to emphasize the caption, "Don't forget Green Vegetables keep you fit", and that of a child with a milk bottle forming its backbone. The campaign with its lectures, posters, leaflets, films, film strips and exhibitions has been conducted continuously since 1939 by the Ministry and has proved most successful in helping to make the whole nation nutrition conscious. The Ministry of Health collaborated in the production of leaflets, emphasizing the dietary needs of expectant mothers and the importance to children of the welfare foods (National Dried Milk, cod liver oil and orange juice). These were distributed in many areas at the Maternity and Child Welfare Clinics, so that mothers might have the information brought to their special notice.

So much indeed is heard about nutrition and our knowledge, both fundamental and applied, of a whole range of sciences dealing with health and food has so vastly expanded over the past four decades, that the layman might begin to wonder how men managed to survive before all this science was known. The answer really is very simple; to be well fed for practical purposes, it is quite sufficient that a diet should be ample, varied and palatable. The more varied the diet, the more likely it is to provide all the sustenance the body needs. It is when shortages occur, either among the people as a whole or among particular groups, that dangers of malnutrition become apparent. Science has enabled us to make the best use of limited resources and can guide us in selecting what should be sought first.

Measuring Food Supplies. For purposes of comparing food supplies in one period with those in another or of one nation with another, it is necessary to find some common measure, but this presents many difficulties owing to the immense number of foods and the fact that so many of them may comprise several types and may be of different grades and qualities.

Individual items such as wheat, rice, sugar, tea, or potatoes can be compared readily enough year by year, or country by country, though even with such apparently homogeneous commodities as these, there may be difficulties in allowing for variation in qualities. Where a food is of a generic type such as meat, there are obvious limitations in statistics compiled by adding say Welsh lamb, ewe mutton, pork, cow beef and veal together in terms of weight, still more if some of the meat is canned or boneless.

To some extent the difficulties can be surmounted for certain groups of foodstuffs by taking such common denominators as "*fat content*" for the butter, margarine, lard and other oils and fats group, or "*milk solids*" for the cream, cheese, liquid milk, condensed milk and milk powder group, or "*edible weight*" for the meat group.

When overall comparisons are required, the difficulties are greater and some common denominator has to be sought which will enable us to add together such diverse commodities as wheat, shell eggs, canned salmon, milk, pork, Camembert cheese, nectarines, coffee, olive oil and oysters. Crude quantities are ruled out at once as it would be meaningless to add say a ton of dried milk to a ton of lettuce. Money value might suggest itself as a way out but immediately difficulties present themselves when comparisons over a period of time are involved, because the value of money itself may have changed in the meantime, or changes may have taken place in the relative prices of imported and home-grown food. Unfortunately in seeking for a common denominator, we are somewhat in the position of the vulgar little boy on Margate Pier who "had no little handkerchief to wipe his little nose", because there is no entirely satisfactory measure and we have to make do as best we can with the calorie.[1] This is the most

[1] The calorie is the unit of energy used in physiology and nutrition. It is actually a kilo-calorie, being equivalent to a thousand of the units defined in the science text-books as the amount of heat required to raise one gramme of water 1 degree Centigrade in temperature.

commonly used unit, and on the whole is open to the fewest objections. Tables are available which enable quantities of foods of all kinds to be readily converted into their calorie equivalents.[1] The values are determined by means of laboratory tests during which the food is burned and its energy-giving value recorded. An ounce of strawberries for example is equivalent to one calorie, an ounce of potatoes to 16 calories, an ounce of sugar to 108 calories, an ounce of margarine to 218 calories and an ounce of lard to 253 calories.

The main limitation of the calorie as a measure of food supplies is that it measures only the energy value of the food and takes no account of the proteins, fats, minerals or vitamins or of qualities such as variety, palatability and all that serves to make food interesting and civilized. A diet of polished rice for example might provide all the calories required for an active life, but it would be woefully deficient in other important nutrients essential to the needs of the human body. Deficiency diseases such as beri-beri or scurvy will occur among people lacking essential nutrients, even though they have a sufficiency of calories. Calories give no measure of the palatability or attractiveness of the diet, and some of the calorie-yielding foods may be too bulky or insufficiently appetizing by themselves to persuade people to consume a sufficiency for full health and activity. This print is stressed in the Report of the British Medical Association's Committee on Nutrition in their discussion on fat in the diet.

"The relatively high calorie value of fats is of special importance when the energy expenditure of the body is large. A diet that is to meet the demands of heavy physical work may be too bulky for those unaccustomed to it, if there is only a small proportion of fat. Apart from their significance as sources of energy, fats influence the nutritional state by providing, in some cases, fat-soluble vitamins and also by facilitating their absorption from other foods."[2]

[1] See for example the Medical Research Council's Memorandum *Nutritive Values of War-time Foods.*
[2] Page 14.

Food, like dress, can be adequate in a purely functional sense, but woefully drab and uninteresting. Seven pounds of potatoes and a pint of milk a day, it has been said, would provide a complete diet, but something more than calories, proteins and vitamins is required for a really satisfactory meal, as the Reverend Sydney Smith fully realized when he defined his idea of heaven as "eating *pâté de foie gras* to the sound of trumpets".

The calorie's usefulness as a common denominator is also somewhat diminished by the fact that small differences occur through the use of different conversion factors. The Food and Agriculture Organization of the United Nations has adopted new factors for the conversion of given weights of food into calories and other nutrients which differ from those used in the British Government's White Papers on Consumption Levels, and in the *Economic Surveys*. These show a somewhat higher calorie figure for total food supplies than the British, though of course the latter are fully comparable for the purpose they have in view, namely comparisons between one year and another. The F.A.O. factors on the other hand have been specially designed for the purposes of international comparisons.

Consumption Levels. The measurement of the nation's food has been the subject of considerable research especially since the food shortages of the war and post-war period brought the matter into prominence, and it is now generally agreed that the most useful measure is provided by consumption levels. Reference has already been made to the subject of consumption levels, but some explanation of the methods used in their construction is now required.

In calculating consumption levels, supplies of food are measured as they enter into civilian consumption at the retail stage or through catering establishments including schools and other institutions. From this data, the *average consumption* per head of the civilian population is worked out for individual foods, groups of food and food in general. To obtain the last-mentioned figure, the total quantities of food both imported and home-grown for the year concerned are divided by the number of consumers, thus giving the quantities per head per annum. The formula for calculating consumption levels is $\dfrac{A + B - C \pm D}{P}$ where A is imported food, B home-grown, C exports of food, D stock changes and P is the civilian population.

Allowances are added to B for the amounts consumed on farms or obtained from gardens, allotments and back-yard poultry. Adjustments are also made for food used as seed or animal feed or for industrial uses.

The figures provided by consumption level studies are of course all *national averages*, and therefore when dealing with the data, it must be borne in mind that they have all the advantages and all the disadvantages inherent in the average. The figures tell nothing about what any particular class or group in the community has consumed, still less what any particular individual has eaten. They represent national averages over a population of some 50 million persons—men, women and children—including heavy manual workers, whose daily calorie requirements may be considerably more than 4,000 a day, sedentary workers requiring perhaps 2,500 calories and infants under a year old whose needs may be less than 1,000 calories a day. Likewise for the other nutrients such as proteins, fat, minerals or vitamins which are included in the official tables, the figures are averages. Requirements vary greatly as between individuals and are not necessarily in the same proportion as they are for calories. A heavy worker for example would only require 0·8 grammes of calcium a day, but a nursing mother would need 2 grammes. A boy aged 16–20 years would need 100 grammes of protein whereas a moderately active man would only require 70.[1]

Though consumption level data do not provide any information about the amount of food eaten by different individuals, social classes or age groups, they are the only available data for the country as a whole, and are the only figures for comparing the overall position in different years. Care must, however, be taken in using the figures so that false con-

[1] *United States National Research Council Recommended Dietary Allowances,* 1945.

clusions are not drawn from them. Owing to the methods
used in measuring supplies, they are not reliable over much
shorter periods than a year. Supplies of a particular commodity do not necessarily come on to the market the same time
each year and it does not follow that a commodity such as
sugar bought say in July is consumed in the same month;
it might be used for fruit preserving and not consumed till
February of the following year. By taking the cycle of the
twelve months, the unevennesses are ironed out and a fair
picture is presented of yearly consumption, especially as the
official figures allow for changes in stocks above retail level.

Food Surveys. To give a complete picture of the food position
in any country, consumption levels need to be supplemented
by further studies of the actual consumption of food as shared
by members of the family in the home and of the food eaten
by individuals. The investigator, however, is on much more
difficult ground when examining these problems than when
dealing with the objective, statistical facts of consumption
levels, food imports or agricultural production. The problems
involve individual preferences, individual needs and family
sharings and in such personal matters, there is room for immense variations and even idiosyncrasies not altogether un-
like those of Jack Spratt and his wife, or the man who according to the old jingle always ate his peas with honey—

> "I eats me peas with honey
> I've done it all me life,
> It makes the peas taste funny
> But it sticks them to the knife."

Consumption level inquiries stop short at the total national
supply of food available at the retail level. They do not show
in any way how the food supply is distributed among families
or individuals. They are national averages and do not therefore show up any uneven distribution among the various
groups in the community. Some of these may be what have
come to be called "vulnerable groups" such as old-age pensioners, families of the unemployed or school children. Though

the national average may be fully satisfactory when measured against the average needs of the community as a whole, it might happen that special groups are for one reason or another obtaining less than their requirements for full health. The causes may be insufficient income to purchase the necessary foods, especially the more expensive "protective foods", lack of knowledge of what constitutes a good diet in relation to their needs, lack of suitable cooking appliances, or inability to undertake the necessary shopping as in the case of some old age pensioners.

The family is the basic unit of the State and within the family the food is shared according to need and tastes. Hence knowledge of a nation's food consumption must depend on obtaining a statistical picture of the food expenditure and consumption of the different kinds of families in the nation. Family budgets have been collected over a good many years, though the material is scattered and rather patchy. None of the surveys made before the Second World War are able to stand up to rigorous statistical cross-examination as to their complete representativeness even of the sections of the community which they purport to represent. This is true even of the Boyd Orr Survey as it included an undue proportion of families in the industrial North, of families with small incomes and relatively large numbers of dependants, though it does broadly show the pattern of food consumption for the period to which it relates. The biggest inquiry into family food consumption is the Food Survey of working-class households undertaken by the Ministry of Food which was commenced in 1941, at first in co-operation with the Ministry of Health. Representative samples of working-class households have been studied continuously at the rate of 600 to 700 households a month with but a few small gaps when special groups were substituted for the general sample. In addition some information has been collected about other groups such as middle-class households, rural families and old age pensioners.

The survey is very detailed and an attempt has been made with considerable success to obtain a representative sample of the households studied, except that perhaps the sample is slightly underweighted with larger families. The method of inquiry is to select working-class wards in each of the towns studied from which households for investigation are selected at random. The households co-operating provide exact information of the amount and cost of all the foods obtained during the week of the investigation. The investigator visits the household at least four times during the period of the survey and checks the information to ensure that all the food eaten in the home is properly recorded, and that details are provided of snacks and packed foods taken to work. Stocks in the larder are weighed at the beginning and end of the survey week. The survey, however, does not take into account any meals purchased and eaten outside the home at works' canteens, restaurants or school refectories. The actual food consumed by members of the family, therefore, would be somewhat higher than shown by the survey.

The survey was undertaken for administrative purposes by the Ministry and the results were not published until 1951 when the first of a series of reports was issued. Some condensed information from the survey is given in the Statistical Appendix (Tables 15 and 16) through the courtesy of the Ministry of Food.

To round off information about food consumption, it is necessary to undertake studies of individual diets. These can take fully into account foods eaten outside the home and can be related to special requirements such as the needs of heavy workers, children or expectant mothers. The technique is difficult and may be tedious to the persons co-operating, because it involves recording and measuring every morsel of food eaten during the period of the investigation. Few individual surveys of any size have been carried out and most of those undertaken relate to children's diets, though there have also been some for schoolboys and women.[1]

[1] See E. M. Widdowson. *A Study of Individual Children's Diets*. Medical Research Council Report, 1947. E. R. Bransby, C. G. Daubney and J. King. *Comparison of Results obtained by Different Methods of Individual Dietary Survey*. British Journal of Nutrition, Vol. 2, No. 2, 1948.

CHAPTER THREE

Food Consumption
between the First and Second World Wars

BETWEEN the two wars, many investigations and surveys relating to food consumption were undertaken and though these were unco-ordinated and for the most part undertaken for special purposes over a somewhat narrow field, they provide much factual information of a kind which was not previously available to anything like the same extent. The increased interest in problems of diet was due to a number of causes. The First World War demonstrated the vulnerable position of Britain in regard to food supplies and the shortages brought about by the German submarine campaign led to rationing and other restrictions which emphasized the gravity of the situation to all. During the nineteen thirties, economic depression and severe unemployment brought into prominence the effects of poverty on nutritional standards. During this period also, a knowledge of nutrition was spreading among the community, and it was coming to be realized that a much higher standard was necessary especially in regard to the more expensive protective foods if the population were to be maintained in full health.

Important contributions on the subjects of food consumption and diet were made by A. W. Flux, A. E. Feavearyear, E. M. H. Lloyd and J. B. Orr. In the following paragraphs, the main facts revealed by these studies are summarized, but the reader interested in this period will find much more detailed information in the papers themselves than can be included here.

Flux compared 1909–13 with 1924–28 and found that the annual cereal consumption per head had fallen by 13 lb., and that of meat by about 1 lb. The consumption of dairy produce and vegetables, however, had gone up while that of fruit showed a considerable increase. He found that after the First World War the average diet had increased in variety.

Feavearyear compared 1932 with the period 1924–27 and found that there had been an undoubted improvement despite the severe industrial depression and heavy unemployment. This he attributed to the advantage which Britain had in obtaining cheap food from abroad. He found that on the average, people were consuming appreciably larger quantities of several of the more important foodstuffs other than bread. Less beef was eaten but the total consumption of meat had increased by 6 per cent as more mutton, lamb and bacon were being bought. The improvement in diet was evidenced by the substitution of butter for margarine and lard. The average person ate 33 per cent more eggs, 10 per cent more sugar and drank 15 per cent more milk. He bought considerably larger quantities of biscuits and cakes from the shops, but his consumption of home-made puddings and pastry was substantially lower. "In short, he moved away from the staple bread-stuffs in the direction of a more varied diet, tending at the same time to substitute factory preparations for home-cooked food."

Lloyd showed that between the 1914–18 war and 1934 there had been a considerable fall in what he called the "nursery group of cereals"—rice, tapioca, sago and arrowroot. "The revolt against the milk puddings of our childhood days appears to have more than halved the national consumption of rice, tapioca and sago. On the other hand, porridge and oatmeal seem to have held their own in spite of the new-fangled breakfast foods." He found that the consumption of bacon and eggs was increasing though the national average was still only about three eggs a head a week. As other investigators had been finding for more than a century, he found for his period as they had found for theirs that sugar consumption was increasing. Indeed it has been said that increasing sugar consumption is an index of growing prosperity, though it is one which the nutritionists regard unfavourably. More valuable from the nutrition point of view was the increasing popularity of fruit and vegetables, those important sources of vitamins and mineral salts. Fruit nearly doubled in consumption and new varieties such as grape-fruit were coming to the tables of ordinary citizens. Vegetable consumption increased by 64 per cent. Milk consumption remained low, but the position in regard to fats improved considerably. The herring, despite its great nutritional value, fell out of favour but tinned salmon was becoming increasingly popular. Lloyd's survey was the first to attempt to apportion the nation's expenditure on food between the different income groups. Dividing the population into six groups, he found that in the lowest group, representing no less than 4½ million persons, the consumption of even the cheapest foods was too low, and altogether insufficient amounts of milk, fruit and vegetables other than potatoes were consumed. In the next two higher groups, representing 18 million persons, the consumption of these foods was below the desirable minimum level.

In Orr's *Food, Health and Income,* published in 1936 and based on Lloyd's data and on investigations carried out by the Rowett Institute and the Market Supply Committee, a new direction was given to the study of food requirements. Instead of considering minimum requirements, which was the basis of previous surveys dealing with poverty, unemployment and nutrition, there was substituted an inquiry into optimum requirements which were defined as "a state of well-being such that no improvement can be effected by a change of diet". This was an interesting change in emphasis and illustrates the trend towards higher standards which was slowly being effected, and the development which was taking place in nutritional science and its applications. The investigation showed that half the population was living at a level of nutrition so high that on the average no improvement would be effected by increasing consumption either in general or of particular foods. Another special feature of this investigation was the grouping of the population according to the income of the family divided by the number of persons in the family. The "higher" income and "lower" income groups in this classification cannot therefore be identified simply with "rich" and "poor" in the generally accepted sense of these terms, since the number of children in the family is the determining factor.

To sum up briefly the results of Orr's investigation, it was found that the nation spent rather less than one-third of the total national income on its food, and that food expenditure amounted to about 9s. a head a week. The consumption of bread and potatoes was practically uniform throughout the different income-level groups, but that of milk, eggs, fruit, vegetables, meat and fish rose with income. Thus in the poorest group the average consumption of milk, including tinned milk, was equivalent to 1·8 pints a head a week whereas in the wealthiest group it was 5·5 pints. The poorest group consumed 1½ eggs a head a week and spent 2·4d. a week on fruit, whereas the wealthiest consumed 4½ eggs and spent 1s. 8d. on fruit.

An examination of the composition of the diet of the different groups shows that the degree of adequacy for health increased as income rose. The average diet of the poorest group, comprising 4½ million people, was, according to the standard adopted, deficient in every constituent examined. The second group, comprising 9 million people, was adequate in protein, fat and carbohydrates but deficient in vitamins and minerals. The group spending 10s. a head on food a week was provided with adequate nutrition and those above had a surplus of all constituents.

To bring the diet of the poor groups up to that which would have been required for full health would have involved increases in consumption of a number of the more expensive foodstuffs, namely milk, eggs, butter, fruit, vegetables and meat varying from 12 per cent to 25 per cent.

In 1938, William Crawford and H. Broadley published under the title of *The People's Food*, the results of an extensive family food survey undertaken during 1936 and 1937, which covered five thousand families of all social classes, living in London and six other large cities which were considered to be representative of economic conditions in the country at that time. The method of investigation adopted was to ask the selected housewives to complete a questionnaire, with the

Food Consumption in the U.K. Average in lb. a head per annum

Commodity	Flux[1]		Feavearyear[2]		Lloyd[3]	M.O.F.[4]
						Pre-war
	1909–13	1924–28	1924–27	1932	1934	average
Wheat flour	211	198			197	195
Potatoes	208	194	187	200	210	176
Vegetables	60	78			98	105
Fruit	61	91	98	106	115	115
Butter	16	16	15½	21¼	25	25
Margarine	6	12	12	9½	8	9
Cheese	7	9	9¾	9¾	10	9
Sugar	79	87	84	92	94	104
Meat[5]	135	134	138	147	143	140

help of the trained investigator, relating to the amounts and values of food purchased in the previous week and the meals consumed the previous day. The method could not attain the accuracy of the Family Food Survey introduced during the Second World War by the Ministry of Food where informants were asked at the beginning of the week to keep a log of all food purchased and consumed, and which also takes into account the change in larder stocks, but the Crawford and Broadley Survey was by far the largest of its kind undertaken before the Second World War, and it provides a great mass of valuable data relating to food habits and standards of food consumption on the eve of the war. For the purposes of the Survey, families were divided into five main social grades,

[1] A. W. Flux. *Our Food Supplies Before and After the War.* J. R. Statistical Soc. XCIII, 538–60. 1930.
[2] A. E. Feavearyear. *The National Expenditure*, 1932. Economic J. XLIV, 33–47. 1934.
[3] E. M. H. Lloyd. *Food Supplies and Consumption at Different Income Levels.* J. Agricultural Economics Soc. IV, 89–120. 1936.
[4] Cmd. 7842. *Food Consumption Levels in United Kingdom.*
[5] Including poultry and rabbits.
The estimates are not strictly comparable one with another as definitions may vary somewhat, but this does not invalidate the general picture presented by the figures.

determined mainly by the income of the chief earner in each household. The Classification was as follows: Class AA (£1,000 and over per annum), Class A (£500 to £999), Class B (£250 to £499), Class C (£125 to £249) and Class D (Under £125). The Survey revealed that weekly *per caput* expenditure on food ranged from 5s. 10d. in the poorest section of the community to 18s. 9d. in the highest group, and that weekly incomes *per caput* ranged from 12s. 6d. in the lowest group to £7 19s. 6d. in the highest. On a *per caput* basis it was found that the lowest income group spent slightly over 55 per cent of income on food, but the percentage decreased as incomes increased until it was only about 16 per cent in the highest group. From the survey data it was estimated that nearly half the population fell below the minimum set out in the British Medical Association's dietary standard in some constituent or another, and the deficiency was particularly marked in respect of Vitamin A and iron. Compared with the diets recommended by the League of Nations Mixed Committee as necessary for optimum health, the shortcomings were even greater, especially as regards vitamin content. The main deficiencies in the national diet were shown to be due to inadequate consumption of "protective" foods (milk, cheese, butter, eggs, green vegetables and fruit) which are rich in vitamins and minerals. Energy foods such as bread, flour, potatoes and sugar were consumed in adequate quantities except by the very poorest classes, and the *per caput* consumption was found to be much the same in all social classes, "indicating that saturation point for these foodstuffs in all sections of the community is almost, if not quite, reached". On the other hand, the consumption of milk and vegetables by all classes, even the wealthiest, lagged behind the desirable level. The authors concluded that in all probability between twenty and thirty million persons were subsisting on diets which were inadequate when compared with the British Medical Association diet. Some eight million of these were spending insufficient on food to purchase the foodstuffs prescribed by the British Medical Association, but an additional twelve to twenty-two millions, though spending weekly on food a sum sufficient to purchase those foodstuffs, were not obtaining the nutritive benefits which the British Medical Association diet would have provided. A certain spartan-like approach to the planning of the meals would have been necessary if this diet were to be followed, as it has to be admitted that the British Medical Association diet is not a particularly appetizing or "interesting" one.

Before the First World War, it had generally been assumed that if people had sufficient food to satisfy their appetites and there was no actual starvation, then they could be considered to be adequately nourished. Since 1909, however, as a result of the discoveries of Gowland Hopkins and others, relating to vitamins, or as Hopkins first referred to them, "the accessory factors of the diet", great strides had been made in the science of nutrition, and during the years between the two wars the relations between diet and health were coming to be much better appreciated. Though the underlying principles were fully appreciated by scientists and other specialists, it was only slowly that the new knowledge spread among the community. Indeed it was still possible in 1950 for Lord Horder's Committee of the British Medical Association on Nutrition to lament "the meagre place which the teaching of nutrition still occupies in the medical student's curriculum, that references to it are desultory and occasional and that there is no systematic teaching of the subject, as there undoubtedly should be".

The new discoveries showed that a diet might be ample enough to satisfy the appetite, but so inadequate from the health-giving point of view as to lead to a constant state of sub-normal health showing itself in such things as slow or stunted growth in children, nervous disorders, impaired digestion and increased liability to infection. In more extreme cases diet, inadequate in essential nutrients, may give rise to specific diseases such as scurvy or rickets. Attention had been directed to the causes of scurvy when long sea voyages were undertaken during the age of maritime exploration in the sixteenth and seventeenth centuries, though the complaint had not been unknown previously among landsmen. The crews of all the great explorers—Magellan, Jacques Cartier,

William Barent—and indeed those of ships engaged on long voyages right down to the eighteenth century were decimated by the disease. It was a long time before the real cause was discovered and it was even longer before the appropriate remedy was introduced.

In 1753, James Lind[1] published *A Treatise on the Scurvy*. This classic work is the most comprehensive study of the disease which has ever been written. Lind recommended oranges and lemons for combating the disease at sea, pointing out at the same time that *dried* vegetables were not effective. Captain Cook discovered by trial and error that fresh fruit and vegetables were effective both as a preventive and a cure. During his second voyage round the world which commenced in 1772, he picked up vegetables and fruit wherever he stopped and on the three years' voyage he lost only one man from scurvy.

In 1795, after unending discussions, the Admiralty added lemon-juice to the sailors' rations. The result was dramatic and by 1806 there was only one case of scurvy in the Naval Hospital at Haslar, whereas formerly there might have been between one and two thousand a year.

Between the two wars, the problem of prescribing a diet adequate for health was approached in several ways. The British Medical Association in 1933, for example, attempted to determine the required mininum weekly expenditure on foodstuffs, by families of varying size, sufficient to maintain health and working capacity, and prepared practical diets which it was believed would meet these demands.

In 1935–36, the Technical Commission of the Health Committee of the League of Nations was asked to define "the nutritional needs of the human being in the course of its development". This Commission also constructed specimen diets. These diets—which were constructed so as to be adequate regardless of cost in contrast to the British Medical Association diets which were "minimum cost" diets—were accepted as a health standard by the Advisory Committee on Nutrition appointed by the Minister of Health in May 1935. This

[1] James Lind, b. 1716, d. 1794. M.D. Edinburgh. Naval surgeon and after 1758 until his death, Physician to the Naval Hospital, Haslar.

Committee drew attention to the lack of detailed studies of the existing standards of nutrition in this country. It therefore recommended that "early steps should be taken to collect family budgets and to undertake dietary surveys on a comprehensive scale".

Recognition of this serious gap in knowledge of the nutritional state of the community led to a number of regional surveys being made in selected areas of the country. These were based on house-to-house visits followed by the statistical examination of the data collected. Some were undertaken by economists investigating problems of poverty, unemployment and social conditions, while others were undertaken by medical officers and others concerned primarily with health. In the former category are the *New Survey of London Life and Labour*, 1929–30 (published in 1932 and planned with a view to a comparison with Charles Booth's classic investigation of the eighteen-nineties), Caradog Jones's Survey of Liverpool in 1929, the same author's Survey of Merseyside, 1929–30, P. Ford's Survey of Southampton, 1931, entitled *Work and Wealth in a Modern Port* and B. S. Rowntree's Second Social Survey of York in 1936 entitled *Poverty and Progress*.

Among the surveys in the second group, namely those undertaken by members of the medical profession, one of the first was an investigation in 1919 by the Scottish Committee for Child Life. It was undertaken with great care and attention to detail and lasted for the best part of five years. This survey, however, was concerned with the intake of proteins, fats and carbohydrates only and it marks the transitional period during which the new knowledge of nutrition was making headway among the scientists, but had not yet spread widely among others. It showed that there was no shortage of food in the areas investigated though poverty forced many to purchase the cheapest foodstuffs available. There was no longer any fear of actual hunger, but lack of the "protective foods" was adversely affecting the health of many children though it was not then recognized that these foods were essential to full health—the retarded growth of children or other manifestations of insufficient consumption of these nutrients being put down to other causes such as bad housing, overcrowding or lack of fresh air and sunshine.

The industrial depression which overshadowed this country after 1929, reduced many areas and numerous families to grim poverty. The unemployed and the lowest wage-earners were only just able to purchase sufficient calories for their needs by eating large amounts of bread and cutting out expenditure on the more expensive foods.

The general picture presented by the surveys made by economists, social workers and medical officers was that poverty was a potent cause in preventing minimum standards of nutrition being attained, and that poverty was likely to be felt with especial severity where there were a number of children in the family. It was also apparent that some of the diets discovered in these surveys among families living below the poverty line were particularly bad, consisting of white bread, margarine, sugar, jam and tea. A poorer diet could hardly be imagined because the foods were devitalized by current methods of manufacture, the white bread for example being made from flour from which much of the valuable nutrients of the wheat had been extracted and, incongruously, fed to animals.

Attention now began to be focused on the need for obtaining precise information about the income levels below which poorer people were obliged to go short of the more expensive "protective foods" such as milk, vegetables and fruit. One of the first investigations devoted to this aspect was one undertaken by G. C. M'Gonigle, the Medical Officer of Health for Stockton-on-Tees.[1]

He was led to this investigation because a number of families who had been moved from slum areas to a new housing estate, all of them poor and many unemployed, had suffered from a rising death rate contrary to what might have been expected. The result of Dr. M'Gonigle's survey led him to conclude that the move to the new estate had involved the families in additional expenditure mainly due to higher rents, and this had been sufficient to reduce their purchases of the

[1] G. C. M. M'Gonigle and J. Kirby. *Poverty and Public Health*, 1936.

more nutritious foods and forced them back on the cheaper foods. Their health thereby was impaired and their resistance to disease lowered.

To sum up the position between the wars, it can be said that though standards of nutrition were unsatisfactory among a large section of the community, and were dangerously low among the unemployed and those with low wages in the depressed areas, there had been by and large a marked improvement since the beginning of the century, as is proved by the steady rise in the *per capita* consumption of meat, milk, fruit and vegetables and the corresponding fall in that of bread, flour and potatoes. Moreover, the admittedly low standards of the worst-fed section of the community were beginning to be measured against a far higher standard than previously. A bare recital of the main statistics will demonstrate this fact. The *per capita* consumption of butter doubled between 1880 and 1936, and that of fruit and vegetables doubled between 1911 and 1936, whereas the *per capita* consumption of wheat flour fell from 252 lb. per annum in 1865 to 197 lb. in 1934 and potatoes from 270 lb. in 1880 to 210 lb. in 1934.[1]

Writing just before the Second World War, Drummond summed up the position at that time as follows:

> "The experts are convinced that the national physique and general health would be greatly benefited by a large increase in the consumption of dairy produce, fruit and vegetables, and it is probable that they will before long express the unanimous opinion that there is a national obligation to see that no child goes without these essential foods because its parents are too poor to buy them. On the other hand, many of those who have studied closely the problem of the future of British agriculture see in the expansion of the production of these very foodstuffs a restoration of prosperity to our farmers."[2]

The main practical steps taken to increase standards of nutrition through direct state action in this period were the

[1] Astor and Rowntree. *British Agriculture.* E. M. H. Lloyd, op. cit.
[2] J. Drummond and A. Wilbraham. *The Englishman's Food To-day.*

Milk-in-Schools Scheme and the School Meals Scheme. The former scheme originated in 1927, when the National Milk Publicity Council introduced a system whereby ⅓ of a pint of milk was provided for school children for 1d. By 1933 nearly a million children were being supplied, but in the following year the cost either to the school authority or the children's parents was reduced to ½d. for ⅓ pint, the difference between this figure and the commercial price of liquid milk being shared by the Government and the newly established Milk Marketing Board. Just prior to the Second World War more than 2½ million children were receiving cheap milk, and over 450,000 were receiving it free. Extra nourishment was also provided through local authorities for expectant and nursing mothers and for children below school age. The school meal system was introduced with the aim of making good deficiencies of food among poor children, and something like 150,000 children in England and Wales before the war were being given a free meal, usually served at mid-day, and consisting of meat, vegetables and puddings.

Developments were also taking place abroad in connection with the feeding of school children, and one of the most interesting which had considerable influence elsewhere was made in a school at Kampens, one of the districts of Oslo in Norway. Instead of a hot mid-day meal, the children were given a breakfast composed of foods carefully selected to supplement the deficiencies of the home diet. There were rolls of wholemeal bread to supply Vitamin B1, and mineral salts lacking in the white bread at home, a good sized pat of butter to provide Vitamins A and D, a hunk of goat's milk cheese and a glass of milk to supply proteins, minerals and vitamins. To provide against mild scurvy, which the lack of fruit in a northern country rendered possible, half an apple or orange, a lettuce salad or a raw carrot was added. When the child had eaten this meal but was still hungry, bread and margarine were provided as a fill-up. The experiment was outstandingly successful and the "Oslo Breakfast" as it has come to be called was adopted in almost every school in Norway, and has had considerable influence outside that country.

CHAPTER FOUR

Food Supply Sources before the Second World War

THE steady growth of population and the rising standard of living which were taking place throughout the nineteenth and the early years of the twentieth centuries steadily increased Britain's dependence on overseas trade for her food supplies. Before the outbreak of the Second World War, Britain had come to depend for two-thirds of her food supplies measured on a calorie basis from overseas sources. Something over twenty-two million tons of food and animal feedingstuffs were imported annually. Though this figure can have little meaning except for shipping purposes, it gives some idea of the absolute size of our import trade in food and feedingstuffs. Our dependence on imports varied considerably as between different foods. Our greatest dependence was for wheat and flour (88 per cent imported), butter (96 per cent) and fats and oils (84 per cent), cheese (76 per cent) and fruit, including tomatoes (74 per cent). On the other hand we produced at home practically all our milk (97 per cent) and about half of our eggs (51 per cent) and meat (49 per cent). Though Britain was predominantly a food-importing country, British agriculture was highly organized and specialized to meet the requirements of the nation for those foods which it was not so economical to import. Thus while the percentage of calories home-produced was only one-third of the total required, the percentage in the case of animal proteins home-produced approximated to two-thirds.

Britain had been for many years the world's greatest importer of food and animal feedingstuffs. Every important food-exporting country in the world, almost without exception, looked to Britain as the main market for its products and our food imports ranged through the alphabet from Almonds to Yeast or from Algerian Wine to Zanzibar Spices. Before the war, no less than a quarter of the annual value of world trade was accounted for by trade in food and feedingstuffs, and of this Britain's share was about 40 per cent. As Britain took the bulk of so many of the foods entering into world trade, she thereby influenced not only trade in these commodities but the production, price and agricultural policies as well as the very livelihood of whole peoples and their States.

Wheat. Total supplies of wheat and flour, averaged over the period 1934–38, were equivalent to about 7¼ million tons of wheat, of which home production accounted for rather less than 23 per cent (i.e. about 1·8 million tons). Something like 40 per cent of these imports came from Canada, 24 per cent from Australia and 15 per cent from the Argentine. Other suppliers were the United States and India.

Coarse grains. In pre-war years, Britain's imports of the coarse grains—maize, barley and oats—which were largely consumed by cattle were about 4 million tons, while some further 3 million tons, mainly oats, were produced at home. Maize was the most important of the imported coarse grains, and amounted to nearly 3 million tons, coming mainly from the Argentine except in those years when the Argentine harvest was poor, when supplies were supplemented by imports from the United States. Barley imports came from the Argentine, the United States, Iraq and Russia; a substantial proportion going to the brewing industry.

In oats there was never a very large international trade as this cereal was mainly consumed on farms or sold locally. Home production provided for the greater part of home consumption and only marginal quantities were imported, coming mainly from Canada. Cattle meal cake was also imported to the extent of some 2 million tons annually, coming mainly from the Argentine, Egypt, India and Burma.

Meat. In the years before the war, Britain consumed some 2·1 million tons of meat a year (carcase weight equivalent), and of this just over half was provided by imports. Beef and beef products came mainly from the Argentine, Australia and New Zealand; mutton and lamb from Australia and New Zealand; and pork from New Zealand, Australia and the

Argentine. British capital and British enterprise had been largely responsible for building up the great meat industries of the Argentine and the Southern Dominions and it was mainly on these areas that we depended for our supplies of imported meat other than bacon. The Argentine provided about 33 per cent of our total meat imports, New Zealand about 18 per cent and Australia 14 per cent.

We consumed before the war some 600,000 tons of bacon (carcase weight equivalent) a year, of which roughly a third was home-produced and two-thirds imported. Of these imports, Denmark supplied about half; Canada being our next largest supplier. Britain was far and away the largest world buyer of meat and bacon, taking something like three-quarters of the world's export trade of some 2 million tons annually.

British imports included both chilled and frozen meat, but the distance which the former could be carried was limited by the fact that chilled meat has to be eaten within a month of slaughtering the animal. Special ships from the River Plate countries were able to do the sea journey to British ports in no more than three weeks, carrying the meat at controlled temperatures just above that at which water freezes. Australia and New Zealand—great pastoral countries like the Argentine —could not supply Britain with chilled meat because the six weeks' journey by sea made it impossible. They were forced to ship their meat frozen with consequent deterioration in its quality.

Chilled meat is much superior to frozen meat, and Argentine chilled meat was rated to taste nearly as good as English home-killed meat. Because of its superior quality, the prices obtained by the Argentine meat exporters were about one-fifth higher than those paid for Australian and New Zealand meat. Britain bought practically the whole supply of chilled meat, only the smallest quantities being purchased by continental European countries.

On the outbreak of war, shipment of chilled meat ceased and has not been resumed.

Dairy Produce. As with meat, a large proportion of international trade in dairy products went to the British market.

Britain imported about four-fifths of the world's exports of butter and about half of those of cheese and eggs. Practically the whole of the butter exports of Australia and New Zealand, and about three-quarters of those of Denmark, were sent to Britain. Likewise nearly all the cheese exports of New Zealand, Canada and Australia were absorbed by the British market.

Milk. Milk was almost entirely produced at home, and indeed milk production was one of the most important activities of British farmers, accounting for a considerable proportion of their total incomes. According to Ministry of Agriculture figures the estimated value of the output of milk and milk products in pre-war years amounted to £80.2 million out of a total gross farm output of £285 million. Something like a third of the milk production went into the manufacture of products such as confectionery and ice cream. This provided a means by which surplus supplies could be absorbed during the flush period, milk being subject to seasonal fluctuations which vary somewhat from year to year. During the summer months (April to September inclusive) the average production may be a quarter more than in the winter, while during the best month of the year, usually May, production may be as much as a half greater than the worst.

Oils and fats. Oils and fats statistics take account only of the "visible" forms as for example, butter, lard, margarine or olive oil. Many other foodstuffs contain a proportion of fat, but as it is not extracted for separate consumption, it is described as "invisible fat". Examples are milk, fish, cheese, peanuts, oatmeal and the covering and marbling of meat. Whether in the "visible" or "invisible" form, fat adds flavour and interest to the meals, and is of great importance in cooking and in making dull foods appetizing. The relatively high calorie value of fats is of great importance when the energy expenditure of the body is large. If there is only a small proportion of fat in the diet, those engaged in heavy physical work may find the necessary food to be too bulky if they are unaccustomed to it. Most people when they have the opportunity and the means, tend to increase their daily consumption of fats such as butter or oil. Those who can do so, would normally, at least in the more temperate climates of the world, obtain 20 to 30 per cent of their energy requirements from oils and fats alone. Weight for weight fat foods yield larger supplies of energy for human beings than do cereals or lean meat.

Oils and fats are derived from a wide range of vegetable and animal sources widely distributed throughout the world. The vegetable fats—copra, groundnuts, sunflower seed, cotton seed, palm oil, palm kernels, soya beans, rapeseed and olive oil—come mainly from tropical or semi-tropical areas, whereas animal fats are produced in the temperate and colder regions. Palm oil and palm kernel are produced mainly in South-East Asia and the Pacific Islands; groundnuts in the East Indies, West Africa, China, India and the U.S.A.; soya beans in the Far East, the U.S.A., South Africa and the East Indies; linseed in India, the U.S.A., the Argentine, the U.S.S.R. and the Baltic States; rapeseed in Europe, India and Malaya; and cotton seed in the U.S.A., the Eastern Mediterranean, India, the U.S.S.R. and Brazil.

"Oils and fats" as the term is understood in commerce, are not confined to edible materials but cover practically all oils and fats derived from vegetable, animal and mineral sources. Some are inedible in the literal sense, as for example, vegetable waxes, volatile vegetable oils used for perfumes, or certain mineral oils which have no food value and are utilized solely for industrial purposes. Others are used only for food but there is no hard and fast distinction as edible oils are often used for industrial purposes such as in making soap, while some initially inedible oils may be converted into food products, or may be used to release oils for food purposes which would otherwise be required for industrial usage. The proportion in which oils and fats are utilized in developed countries is roughly two-thirds edible and one-third industrial usage, but in the under-developed countries the inedible proportion is smaller.

The main end-usages on the edible side are margarine, butter, lard, compound lard, cooking fats, dripping, cooking oils and salad oils. The main inedible usages are for soap

making, and drying oils (mainly linseed oil) for paint and lino-
leum manufacture.

Oils and fats are to a considerable extent inter-changeable
states as all fats change to oils at a temperature above their
melting points, and all fatty oils solidify into fats at lower temperatures. All oils, however, are not fatty, but those which are
non-fatty have no bearing on the food situation except in so
far as they can be used to replace fatty oils for industrial purposes as for example in the manufacture of detergents.

The trend in utilization of oils and fats during the present
century has been away from inedible and towards edible usage.
Modern techniques of de-odorization, refining or hydrogena-
tion have permitted many materials formerly classed as inedible to be used in the manufacture of edible oils and fats.
The use of mineral products in the manufacture of synthetic
detergents has recently reduced to some extent the demand
for oils and fats for these purposes.

Marine oils in the form of whale oil and seal oil from the
Antarctic and the Arctic, accounted for 650,000 tons pre-war,
but the rate of capture was so high that the whales were being
gradually exterminated.

Vegetable oils are consumed largely in the form of margarine
and cooking fats. The world's trade in vegetable oils was
largely a movement of supplies from tropical and semi-
tropical countries to Western Europe and North America.
Britain, in order to maintain her high level of fat consumption,
relied to a great extent upon imported supplies.

Sugar. Sugar is obtained commercially from two sources,
namely sugar cane and sugar beet which give identical refined
products. Sugar cane is a tropical plant, the main pre-war
producers being the West Indies, Brazil, Cuba, Java, the
Philippines, Formosa, India, Queensland and South Africa.
Sugar beet is grown in temperate climates and was extensively
cultivated, pre-war, in Germany, Czechoslovakia, the U.S.A.,
France and the U.S.S.R.; several of these countries developing
production by means of subsidies. Before the war, most of
the world's trade in sugar was in the form of raw cane sugar,
whereas beet sugar production tended to be consumed in the

country of origin though some sugar exports were provided by the U.S.S.R., Poland and Czechoslovakia. Britain, though consuming nearly twice as much sugar per head as Continental Europe, depended to a far greater extent on imported sugar than did any other European country. Some of the raw sugar, however, was re-exported in the form of refined sugar. In pre-war days this country produced at home somewhat less than 20 per cent of her requirements.

Before the war, the biggest importers of sugar were the U.S.A., Britain and Japan in that order and each sought to obtain its supplies from the areas under its influence. Shortly after the First World War, each of the great importing countries began to afford preferences to the areas under their influence. India rapidly became self-sufficient, and countries like Cuba and Java, which were low-cost producing areas, soon found that they could not sell all their sugar because effective demand was being restricted by high import duties. World production began to exceed demand, stocks rose, prices fell and production had to be curtailed. The severe economic depression after 1929 restricted the demand for sugar even further, and in 1931 the Chadbourne Agreement between Cuba, Java, Peru and five European countries was signed. This agreement aimed at reducing production by 50 per cent, but its objects were not attained because countries outside the Agreement increased their production. This was followed in 1937 by a comprehensive international agreement which covered 90 per cent of the world's sugar trade. Each exporter was given a quota of what he could place on the free market. Both price and demand, however, remained low, and in Java, in 1939, less than half the number of factories which had operated in 1929 were functioning.

Summary. Britain's position on the eve of the Second World War, was unique among the nations of the world, in that she depended on imports for the greater part of her food, and was quantitatively by far the largest world buyer of foods of all kinds. International trade was the very condition of her existence, whereas to most if not all other countries, foreign trade in food was only a means to augment their own domestic harvests when these were below average, or a means of gaining products which could not be grown in their own climates. Between the two world wars Britain gained greatly as a result of the movement of the terms of trade in her favour, owing to the relative decline in the advantage of primary producers. Her food position was, however, vulnerable in war.

CHAPTER FIVE

Effects of the Second World War
on Britain's Sources of Food Supplies

THE war largely upset the pattern of Britain's sources of food supply, and necessitated a transfer from former areas of supply of certain commodities to new sources, and for other foods at any rate it largely altered the balance of the sources of supply. In the war years, the main problem for Britain was not world shortage of supplies or any difficulties in currency after Lend-Lease was negotiated; it was largely a matter of shipping availabilities. If the ships were available, the food could be obtained. It was after the war that world shortages and currency complications began seriously to affect Britain's food supplies. The main changes during the war were that Britain lost supplies from Europe and, after the Japanese conquests, from South-East Asia while during the later stages of the war supplies from Australia and New Zealand were diverted to feed troops in the Pacific.

To make good the losses of imports, greater reliance had to be placed on the United States and Canada. The changes in supply sources which occurred are illustrated by the diagrams on pages 58 and 59 and in Table 2 of the Statistical Appendix.

Britain's dependence on overseas trade for food was both a source of strength and a source of weakness during the war. As it is pointed out in the Official History of the War, Britain's advantage was great in being able to draw upon distant lands, but in earning it she had chosen to live dangerously. Britain obtained much greater benefits from the production of the Americas and the Argentine than Germany ever did during the war from her more secure but limited advantages in having over-run most of Europe and from which she drew reluctant tribute. "Germany was creating in Europe a 'new order' largely subservient to German military command; but the international economic order to which the United Kingdom belonged was still in large measure governed by the notions of economic self-interest held by the individual communities participating in it. Britain might be granted some privileges of deferred payment, her merchant fleet might be reinforced by ships of other nations; but until the coming of Lend-Lease the strength that she could draw from overseas was sharply limited by her own capacity to pay and to ship."[1]

During the first six months of the war, the so-called "phoney stage", there was little interference with shipping, and Britain's food imports continued to arrive even from Denmark and the other Baltic States. Between April and the end of June 1940, however, Germany over-ran Denmark, Norway, the Netherlands, Belgium, Luxembourg and France. In these few months, supply sources which used to provide some 1¾ million tons of food annually were lost, though temporarily there was some compensation as the result of the diversion to British ports of about a million tons of food which was on its way to other European countries. The loss of European sources of supply affected especially imports of bacon and ham, eggs, butter, condensed milk and milk powder.

When in June 1940, Italy entered the war on the enemy's side, ships had to be diverted from the Suez Canal and the Mediterranean route to the longer route round the Cape. The shipping position also deteriorated greatly because of the U-boat campaign which had become more intense, and partly because the convoy system, which had to be introduced to frustrate the attacks, meant slower voyages, as the speed of a convoy is regulated by the speed of the slowest ship sailing with it. Difficulties also resulted as ships in home waters and the ports were subject to air attacks from bases across the Channel. In addition, the needs of the armed forces and the supply requirements of the munition industries at home necessitated the diversion of ships from the carriage of food to the transport of other cargoes. Refrigerator ships, because of their speed, were transferred to naval duties, and this had a serious effect on the import of meat. As a result, the meat ration had

[1] W. K. Hancock and M. M. Gowing. *British War Economy*. Page 103.

THE CHANGE IN SOURCES

(Pre-war figures are

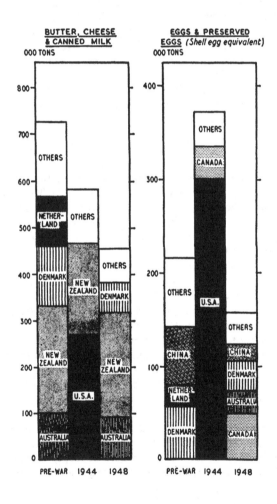

BUTTER, CHEESE
& CANNED MILK
000 TONS

EGGS & PRESERVED
EGGS *(Shell egg equivalent)*
000 TONS

OF U.K. FOOD IMPORTS
average of years 1934–38)

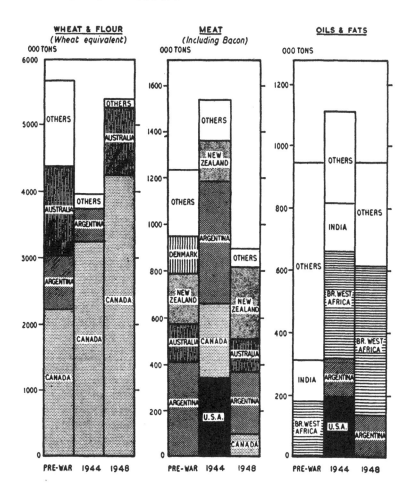

WHEAT & FLOUR
(Wheat equivalent)

MEAT
(Including Bacon)

OILS & FATS

to be halved at the beginning of 1941, and this was the more severely felt as at the same time the supply of fish was seriously reduced because most of the trawler fleet had been requisitioned and enemy action interfered with fishing in certain waters.

The loss of food supplies from Europe meant that alternative sources of supply had to be sought. More bacon and cheese were obtained from Canada and more butter from New Zealand, but these extra supplies were not enough to replace the losses, and no ready alternative sources of supply were available for eggs and canned milk at that time.

Throughout 1941, shipping losses were heavy as the full measure of the submarine menace had not been taken, nor had methods been adopted to frustrate the attacks. The food import programme had to be curtailed and imports were restricted to essential foods. In the spring of 1941, the nation's diet dropped to the lowest average for any quarter for the whole war period. There were serious shortages of meat, cheese, milk and fish, while many of the less important foods such as jam or onions were difficult to obtain and imported fresh and canned fruits practically disappeared. The outlook at that time was grim indeed as it was becoming apparent that the approaching exhaustion of Britain's dollar resources might prevent the purchase of much-needed foods from the United States. In the event, however, this contingent catastrophe was averted by the passage of the Lend-Lease Act in the United States: This Act enabled Britain to obtain sorely needed supplies of valuable foodstuffs which could not be obtained elsewhere. In the summer of 1941, supplies of cheese, lard and canned goods began to arrive and were followed later by supplies of bacon, dried egg and canned milk. By the late autumn, stocks of canned meat and canned fish had been accumulated in sufficient quantity to allow a limited distribution to be effected. By 1943, Lend-Lease supplies amounted to over 14 per cent by value of our total food imports.

Lend-Lease Arrivals of Food in the U.K.

Year	Thousand tons	Per cent of Total Arrivals
1941	1,073	7·3
1942	1,427	13·7
1943	1,705	14·6
1944	1,280	11·7

Note.—1943 was a year of 53 weeks.
Source.—*How Britain was Fed in War-time.*

British food supplies took another knock in December 1941, when Japan attacked Pearl Harbour and the war spread to the Pacific. Britain's normal sources of supply of sago, tapioca and pepper were cut off as were also about half her pre-war supply sources of copra and about one-third of those of coconut oil. The conquest of Indo-China, Thailand and Burma by the Japanese deprived Britain of 80 per cent of her pre-war supplies of rice and the occupation of the Netherlands East Indies meant the loss of valuable supplies of sugar, tea and vegetable oils.

The opening-up of hostilities in the Pacific brought with it serious dangers to the passage of food ships travelling across the Indian Ocean from Australia and New Zealand. It became necessary also to provide food for the armed forces engaged in the Pacific theatre of war, and this meant the diversion of food cargoes, particularly of meat and dairy produce, from Australia and New Zealand, to provide supplies for American and Imperial troops engaged in the Pacific struggle. In compensation, however, larger supplies of food under the Lend-Lease arrangements were sent to this country from the United States. "Food," said President Truman in his Nineteenth Lend-Lease Report to Congress (May 1945), "has been one of the most important items provided by Australia and New Zealand. By 1 January 1945, we have received from these two countries, 2,635 million lb. of food for the U.S. forces in the Pacific."

During 1942, it became necessary to economize as much as possible in the amount of shipping space used for food transport, and with this end in view, the extraction rate of flour, already increased to 75 per cent of the wheat grain from the 70 per cent or less of pre-war days, was further raised in March 1942, to 85 per cent, which meant that out of every 100 tons of wheat imported, 85 tons of flour were obtained instead of the 70 tons or less in pre-war days. The increased extraction rate was advantageous nutritionally, as bread made from the high extraction rate flour retained important minerals and vitamins hitherto lost in the milling process. Against this gain, however, there had to be offset a loss in the quantity and quality of feedingstuffs for animals, which are made from the residue from the flour mills. Later in the year it was decided to attempt to eke out the wheat supply by mixing a proportion of barley and small quantities of rye and oats with the wheat flour, but this policy was abandoned after a few months' trial. Publicity campaigns were also initiated with the object of encouraging the eating of potatoes in place of bread. Great efforts were also made to impress on the public the importance of preventing any waste of food, especially bread.

By the end of 1942, food stocks had fallen to the minimum safe working levels, and it was becoming difficult to maintain an even distribution of some foods. During the war years, the problem of food stocks was complicated by the necessity of providing for inevitable delays in shipping and in port clearances and for the dispersal of stocks to guard against the dangers of heavy air raids or the danger of invasion. Food stocks at the outbreak of war stood in general at normal peacetime levels except for certain purchases of wheat, sugar and whale oil by the Government in 1938–39 under the Essential Commodities (Reserves) Act, 1938. For the first few months of the war, some inroad was made into stocks, but from the end of 1939 to the end of 1941 stocks under the control of the Ministry of Food were increased. In 1942 these stocks had to be distributed to the amount of some 700,000 tons. In 1943 imports increased, as did the contribution from home agriculture, and it was possible to increase the Ministry of Food's controlled stocks to more than 6½ million tons by the end of

1943. About two million more tons of food were imported than were consumed during the year, and some of this could have been used to improve standards of consumption, but it was felt that every ship might be needed for forthcoming military operations, and that the liberation of Europe would require Britain to provide food for the liberated countries. By the end of September 1945, Britain was able, as a result of this policy, to make available practically a million tons of food to the United Nations Relief and Rehabilitation Administration, to SHAEF and to the Governments of those countries who were making their own arrangements to purchase supplies.

Towards the end of 1944, Britain's food imports began to fall below consumption requirements owing to the drain on shipping resources which resulted from military operations, and this fall continued after the cessation of hostilities, because of the need to ship supplies to liberated Europe. By that year, the pattern of Britain's food imports had undergone a marked change. The changes affected both the quantity of imports and the sources of supply. Imports of some commodities had increased. Thus more oils and fats were being imported, Egypt being replaced by British West Africa and substantial quantities coming from the Argentine and French Africa. Meat imports had gone up by one-fifth with the Argentine, still the main single source of supply. The United States and Canada had supplanted Australia, New Zealand and Denmark as the next most important suppliers. In the main, however, imports showed a reduction.

Wheat and flour imports fell to two-thirds of the pre-war average though Canada's share increased by 50 per cent. Imports of animal feedingstuffs fell to one-twentieth of pre-war, and those of rice and similar products fell to one-tenth. Sugar imports fell to one-half; Cuba and San Domingo being the chief sources of supply. Imports of fruit and vegetables were only one-quarter of what they had been in pre-war days, while dairy produce imports fell off by a quarter though the United States was making good most of the losses from European exporters.

British Agriculture during the War. There was a considerable expansion in home agriculture during the war years, as British farmers were called upon to make good some of the deficiencies which resulted from the loss of import supplies. But not only was agriculture required to make an all-out effort, it was also required to make considerable changes in the direction of its activities, so that its contribution might help to reduce the volume of shipping space required and provide foods essential to the maintenance of nutritional standards.

There was little scope for increasing output by bringing new land into cultivation, for almost all cultivable land was already in agricultural use. Reclamation of waste land therefore made only a small contribution to the drive for increased agricultural production, and was in fact more than offset by losses from land turned over to military uses, aerodromes and other non-agricultural uses. The problem was one of increasing the output of human food from existing farmlands and this was tackled in two ways, namely by increasing the actual physical yield of the land (largely by ploughing up grasslands) and by increasing the proportion of crops available for direct human consumption. The production of wheat, potatoes, sugar beet, vegetables and fodder crops was all substantially increased. By 1943, which was the peak of the home agricultural effort, the production of wheat and potatoes had been doubled, the production of oats was 60 per cent greater, that of other grains more than doubled, and that of fodder crops had increased by nearly a third. Sugar beet production was up by 40 per cent.[1]

The number of livestock declined greatly as a result of expansion in farm crops grown for direct human consumption, the ploughing-up of grasslands and the severe reduction which took place in the import of animal feedingstuffs. The number of pigs fell to half what it had been before the war, and poultry were reduced by over 20 per cent, though as might be expected the number of back-yard and domestically kept poultry increased. Pigs and poultry compete with human beings for cereals, and it was impossible to import adequate grain to

[1] See Tables 3 and 4 in the Statistical Appendix, for figures relating to agricultural production.

maintain them in pre-war numbers; the greater part of the fodder crops grown at home was utilized to maintain the production of milk. In consequence of the policy of giving first priority to the production of milk, dairy cattle increased in numbers over the period 1939 to 1945 from 3·9 million to 4·3 million, that is by about 10 per cent, and cattle as a whole increased from 8·9 million in 1939 to 9·4 million in 1945. Maintenance of milk supplies, even though dairy cattle were given priority, set farmers a difficult problem because in 1939 curtailment of imports forced dairy farmers to abandon their pre-war system of feeding their animals on cheap imported feedingstuffs. At first, production and yields per cow went down, reaching their lowest level in 1941. Thereafter they gradually rose. In contrast to the policy of maintaining the cattle population, it was found impossible to maintain that of sheep, whose numbers fell by nearly a third, from about 30 million in 1939 to 20 million in 1945.

Home production of food before the war contributed about 31 per cent of the total calories and about 44 per cent of the total proteins, consumed by the people of this country. By 1943 the percentage for calories had increased to as much as 43 per cent, despite the reductions in the amount of feedingstuffs imported. In the case of proteins, the percentage home-produced in 1943 had risen to a little over 50 per cent, but this increase was only obtained by a proportionately higher increase in vegetable proteins to compensate for a reduction in animal proteins due to a reduction in home-produced meat. Whereas in pre-war years the percentage of animal protein produced by home agriculture was 62 per cent, this had fallen to 52 per cent in 1943. The percentage of home-produced vegetable protein on the other hand had risen from 24 per cent to 50 per cent.

Production fell off somewhat after 1943 and the proportion of home-produced food was 41 per cent in 1945, the biggest fall being that of wheat.

It might seem that an increase of 12 per cent in the proportion of home-produced food is not a very great increase in view of the effort which went into agricultural production during the war, but it has to be remembered that Britain is a very densely populated country with some 50 million persons to be fed. This increase of 12 per cent in the proportion of calories produced at home represented an increase of a third of the pre-war production.

CHAPTER SIX

Food Consumption during the Second World War

DURING the war, drastic changes in the pattern of food consumption were forced on this country owing to the shortage of shipping. Nevertheless, food supplies were maintained at a level which provided, except possibly in 1940 and 1941, a sufficiency to eat for all, though the regimen was of a spartan nature, and many of the more attractive and desirable foods were severely rationed or disappeared entirely. The energy value of the nation's diet never fell as much as 7 per cent below the pre-war level and indeed in 1944, by which year Lend-Lease had helped to build-up supplies, rose to slightly more than it was in the pre-war period. Expressing the energy-value of the diet in terms of calories per head per day, this averaged 3,000 calories in pre-war days, but never fell below 2,800 calories during the war, and rose to 3,010 calories in 1944. There was on the other hand a considerable drop in the consumption of animal proteins during most of the war years, but this was more than made good by an increase in vegetable proteins, as will be seen from Table 9 in the Statistical Appendix. The consumption of fats remained below the pre-war rate throughout the war by amounts varying from 7 per cent to 13 per cent.

Maintenance of this degree of sufficiency was only made possible by drastic changes in the composition of the diet, as will be seen from Table 10 in the Statistical Appendix. Wartime diets were monotonous and palatability was reduced much below that to which the people of this country had become accustomed. At one time, indeed, it seemed that even more drastic changes in the diet would be forced on the nation. After Dunkirk, the prospect of a siege economy had to be faced, and the Government therefore appointed a committee of scientists to advise on a diet which would require a minimum of imports. This Committee reported that all the nutritional needs of the nation, including calories, proteins, fats, minerals and vitamins, could be provided by a diet of wholemeal bread, oatmeal, fats, milk, potatoes and vegetables. Wheat and fats would have to be imported, but the scientists thought that all the other foods in the list could be produced at home to meet minimum needs of the whole population. It is doubtful if this could have been implemented in practice, but it was never necessary as events turned out for Britain to have to face such drastic measures.

Throughout the war, meat, fish, butter, eggs, fruit and sugar were scarce, and deficiencies in these foods had to be made good by the consumption of larger quantities of bulky and less attractive foods such as cereals and vegetables. From about 1941, potatoes, which are almost entirely a home-grown crop, became a much more important element in the nation's food supplies, average consumption rising from the 176 lb. a head pre-war to 275 lb. in 1944 though falling to 260 lb. in 1945. Potatoes were eaten to make good, in part, the losses resulting from reduced supplies of other foods, and being unrationed right through the war they, along with bread, acted as buffer foods, enabling people to obtain additional energy-giving food over and above the rationed foods. By the end of the war, the consumption of potatoes was nearly 60 per cent above that of pre-war days.

In the winter of 1941–42, the Government instituted a vigorous propaganda campaign to encourage the consumption of more potatoes and to promote their use in place of other foods. The public was exhorted to serve potatoes for breakfast on three days a week, to make potatoes a main dish on one day a week, and to refuse second helpings of other foods until they had had more potatoes. Suggestions and recipes were also published for serving potatoes in other ways than "plain boiled".

The importance of the potato in the war-time economy of Britain would be hard to exaggerate, for in two world wars it has provided a life-line for the British public. Output of potatoes was greatly expanded in both wars and potatoes were used to replace imports of other foods and provided an acceptable substitute for bread, which, otherwise, would have had to be eaten in greater quantities than it was during either of the world wars. In the following table the average weekly consumption of potatoes is set out in a form enabling comparison to be made of the increases in consumption as the wars progressed. In both wars, consumption had increased greatly by the end of the period of hostilities.

Weekly average consumption of potatoes in lb. per head

	Pre-war	War Years					
		First	Second	Third	Fourth	Fifth	Sixth
First World War	3·7	4·3	4·4	4·1	3·8	5·3	—
Second World War	3·4	3·2	3·6	4·3	4·8	5·3	5·0

As well as eating more potatoes, people ate more bread during the war, and the consumption of flour rose from 195 lb. a head per annum in pre-war years to 237 lb. in 1941. Thereafter it fell back slightly, but rose to 241 lb. a head in 1945, when fewer potatoes were being eaten.

By 1945, the consumption of oatmeal, barley and breakfast cereals had increased considerably, though of course these cereals have never had in the present century anything like the importance of wheat flour in the national diet. Consumption of these minor cereals rose from about 8 lb. a head per annum in pre-war years to 15 lb. in 1945. In contrast the cereal group comprising rice, starch, tapioca and sago was affected by supply difficulties, and their consumption fell heavily after 1942, with supplies of tapioca and sago practically disappearing. Rice also nearly disappeared after 1944, when the effects of the Japanese occupation of South-East Asia began to be felt.

Consumption of vegetables increased from 108 lb. a head pre-war fairly steadily year by year until it was 127 lb. in 1945; the largest increase being registered by cabbages and carrots. On the other hand, the supplies of fruit of all kinds (fresh, canned and dried) fell off and were only 91 lb. a head in 1945 as compared with 141 lb. pre-war.

A Vitamin Welfare Scheme was introduced in December 1941 to make up for probable shortages of vitamins in the diet of young children arising from lack of fruit, particularly oranges, and the shortages of butter and eggs. Under the scheme, blackcurrant syrup or purée and cod liver oil were provided free of charge for children up to two years of age. In April 1942 the blackcurrant products were gradually replaced by Lend-Lease orange juice and a charge was made for them. Ultimately, the scheme was linked up with the National Milk Scheme, when any expectant mother or child under five years of age who had cheap or free milk became automatically entitled to cheap or free supplies of orange juice and cod liver oil. Vitamin A and D tablets were provided as an alternative for expectant mothers.

The dairy products group, excluding butter, showed an increase amounting to 31 per cent over pre-war in 1943, but was slightly lower in 1944 and 1945 at 28 per cent and 30 per cent respectively above pre-war. This group includes liquid milk, cream, cheese and evaporated, condensed and dried milk. Condensed milk, including both the full cream sweetened and machine-skimmed sweetened types, fell to about one-quarter of the supplies available before the war, and cream disappeared entirely, as its production was prohibited after 1940 and was not permitted again until 1951, and then only for a short time. Dried and evaporated milk increased by nearly a half, but their production was not at any time, either before or during the war, very large a proportion of the total milk supply.

The largest and most important increase in the dairy products group was in liquid milk consumption, which had increased to as much as 44 per cent above pre-war in 1945. Milk production was given priority over other forms of livestock farming, owing to its importance to national health, and every effort was made to secure that the milk went to those whose need was greatest by means of the National Milk Scheme and the Milk-in-Schools Scheme.

The National Milk Scheme was introduced in July 1940 to provide for every child under five years of age and for every expectant mother, a pint of milk daily at 2d. a pint, instead of 4½d., the price then ruling in most districts. Where the family income was below a certain level, the milk was provided free of cost. In 1940 somewhat over 2½ million consumers benefited from the scheme, but by 1944 practically 4 millions were participating in it. The proportion of consumers obtaining free milk was 30 per cent in 1940, but by 1944 this had fallen to 3 per cent owing to the general rise in family incomes during the war. The Milk-in-Schools Scheme went back well before the war, but during the war years it was greatly expanded.

Extra milk was not provided for old people largely because of the numbers involved, there being some 5 million persons in the "over 65" age group. It was held to be more important for children and expectant mothers because it contains calcium and acts as a bone builder.

Butter, which normally for statistical purposes is included in the oils and fats group, showed a drastic fall, supplies being in 1945 little more than a third of pre-war. Cheese consumption, on the other hand, rose to 59 per cent above pre-war in 1942, but gradually declined until in 1945 it was only 10 per cent above pre-war. The quality, however, was much inferior, and the noble cheeses such as Stilton and Gloucester disappeared from our tables, being replaced by a standard product which was familiarly described as the "mouse-trap" variety.

Falls in *per capita* consumption took place in meat, fish, oils and fats, sugar, pulses and nuts, and tea, though coffee showed a considerable increase, no doubt because it is an acceptable substitute to many persons for tea, supplies of which were some 12 per cent below pre-war in 1945, and had been even lower in 1943 and 1944.

The meat group reached its lowest point for the war years in 1941, when it was not much more than three-quarters of the pre-war consumption. It was, however, only 12 per cent below in 1944, but fell again in 1945 to 21 per cent below.

6

There were very considerable variations in the composition of the totals; mutton and lamb supplies were well maintained, but pig meat, including bacon and ham, was very greatly reduced. The supplies of canned meat increased very considerably. Egg consumption, including dried and liquid egg, was lowest in 1941, being then 24 per cent below pre-war and highest in 1945 at 7 per cent above pre-war. Shell eggs decreased greatly but dried egg supplies, practically unknown before the war, had increased steadily during the war.

The consumption of margarine doubled during the war, being used as a substitute for butter, which fell to about a third of pre-war. Taken together, butter and margarine supplies were only about three-quarters of pre-war.

Sugar and syrup supplies were considerably reduced during the war, being 35 per cent below pre-war in the years 1941 to 1943, but improving somewhat in 1944 and 1945, when they were about 30 per cent below pre-war consumption.

Apart from changes in the major foods, there was also a marked diminution in many of the minor foods such as cream, ice cream, olive oil, salad creams or table jellies. These, though individually less important, collectively enable considerable diversity to be given to meals based on the same main dishes. Where these small items did not disappear, they were frequently in very short supply or were only available in much poorer quality, sometimes indeed only in substitute form. Cakes and biscuits fell off greatly in quality, jam was less attractive, milk chocolate disappeared, and so on through a long list, there was a falling away from pre-war standards.

To sum up the position during the war, it may be said that apart from the increase in the *per capita* consumption of liquid milk, and that of cheese, the trend was towards an increase in the consumption of those foods which had been declining in popularity in the years preceding the war when improvements in the standard of living were leading to greater variety and attractiveness in the diet of the ordinary person. This is statistically illustrated by the fact that whereas before the war, 34 per cent of total calorie supplies were obtained from grain products and potatoes, these provided 44 per cent in

1945. Supplies of total protein increased substantially, except in 1940, though the composition of the total changed; animal proteins declined, but were more than made good by vegetable proteins. The mineral and vitamin content of the average diet also increased substantially, except perhaps for ascorbic acid and for Vitamin A. The picture which emerges from a study of consumption level data is confirmed broadly by the results of the National Food Survey of the Ministry of Food (see page 190) and other inquiries.

Two important changes in the pattern of the nation's food consumption which took place during the war years require to be stressed in any assessment of the relative positions before and after the war, as they have helped to transform nutritional standards in this country. The first change is that which has been due to our increased knowledge of nutritional science and the practical applications which have been made of this recently acquired knowledge. Already before the war, this knowledge had begun to permeate down to the general public, and administrators were beginning to frame policies which took account of it. During the war, administrative action and government propaganda powerfully reinforced the movement, and as a result, despite all the difficulties of the food supply situation, actual improvements were effected in the diet of the country. Among the practical measures taken by the government to raise the dietary standard of the nation, or that of special groups, there may be specially mentioned the National Milk Scheme, the extended Milk-in-Schools Scheme, the raising of the extraction rate of wheat and the propaganda in favour of increased consumption of vegetables. To supply nutrients which otherwise would have been deficient in the austere war-time diets, the government on the advice of the scientists introduced such measures as the fortification of bread with calcium, the vitamin scheme and the fortification of margarine with Vitamins A and D.

Important contributions were also made to national well-being by the provision of industrial canteens, British Restaurants and school meals.

The second change was that of a greater degree of equality

among all classes. The extension of rationing together with price controls meant that the consumption of the available foods became less and less unequal. Backed by high wages, full employment and food subsidies, it became possible for families in the lowest income groups to obtain many essential nutrients, the pre-war consumption of which among the poorer families was low. On the other hand, the consumption of certain foods by those better-off was reduced as compared with their pre-war standards, and there was less room for the exercise of choice except in so far as family sharing mitigated the rigidity of the distribution.

During the war, the health of the nation was surprisingly well maintained and mortality data show that after an initial set-back in 1940–41, the pre-war downward trends were continued. Improvements were shown in all the main mortality indices, including infant, post-natal, neo-natal and maternal mortality. The mortality rate for the age groups over 45 actually showed a considerably accelerated rate of improvement over the pre-war improvement, and was probably due to the advances which had been taking place in medical science.

It is not possible to assess to what extent, if any, the war-time improvement in mortality rates has been due to changes in diet, because mortality and morbidity are affected by many factors. There have been several notable medical discoveries over the last decade or so, the application of which to clinical practice has had a great influence in reducing death rates.[1] This at least we can say, that at any rate the war-time diet was sufficiently nourishing so as not to counteract progress in other directions.

---

[1] A valuable discussion on the whole subject will be found in the Report of the Committee on Nutrition issued by the B.M.A. in 1950. Chapter IV. "Clinical Assessment of the Nation's Health in Terms of Nutrition."

CHAPTER SEVEN

Food Controls, Rationing and Price Regulation

The Ministry of Food. The Ministry of Food which was established on 8 September 1939, and which has now become a permanent Department of State, is one of the largest trading organizations in the world, having an annual turnover of something like 1½ thousand million pounds a year. The Ministry is responsible for the procurement of foodstuffs from home and overseas and it controls within this country the processing, manufacture and distribution of foodstuffs of every kind. The Ministry is also responsible for the maintenance and improvement of food standards, and carries out research into methods of preparing, marketing and preserving foodstuffs as well as advising the public on the best methods of cooking and preparing the available foodstuffs. Among the other functions of the Ministry are the storage and transport of foodstuffs, licensing and rationing, control of prices and profit margins, determination and payment of subsidies, provision of statistical information, enforcement of food regulations, salvage, control of ancillary materials and representation on international organizations concerned with food.

The nucleus for a Ministry of Food existed on the outbreak of the Second World War within the Board of Trade in the Food (Defence Plans) Department which had been set up in 1936. This was a small organization, staffed mainly by officials who had experience of food control in the First World War, and the impulse to its establishment had come largely from Sir William Beveridge, a one-time Permanent Secretary of the Ministry of Food of the First World War who had been called in to serve as Chairman of a group of officials advising on the technical problems of food rationing. Sir William Beveridge laid down four essential conditions for effective food control. These were: (1) Appointment of a Food Controller with full powers as from the first day of war; (2) Determination of a feeding policy for adequate total supply at all stages of a possibly protracted war; (3) Preparation in advance of plans for the control of each essential food and (4) Planning steps to meet air attack.

At the time of the Munich Crisis none of these conditions had been met, but when war broke out a year later, preparations under all the headings except the second were well in hand. "The Food Controller was ready to take over; commodity controls were ready and ration books printed; plans were prepared to meet the expected air attack. The 'feeding policy', however, had not been thought out beforehand. It was to emerge gradually, even reluctantly, under the pressure of events."[1]

Rationing. Food rationing was introduced in January 1940 and by the end of 1943 most foods were rationed or controlled in one way or another. A system of straight rationing was adopted for meat, bacon, fats, sugar, cheese, preserves and tea, and this has continued in operation throughout the post-war years, except for the de-rationing of preserves, and the freeing of imported fancy cheeses. Straight rationing is the simplest method of rationing since the consumer is registered with and tied to a particular retailer, who in turn receives a permit from a designated wholesaler, based on the number of his registered customers. From the administrative point of view, it has the advantage of providing advance information to the controlling authority as to each retailer's requirements. It also reduces clerical work and the need for records and checking.

Straight rationing was supplemented by a points rationing scheme which was adopted for the rationing of less important foods in order to give more flexibility by providing each consumer with the opportunity of making a choice between a large number of foods, each valued on a points system which was varied from time to time on the basis of coupon demand and the supply of the particular food. Among the foods which were included under the points system were canned meats,

[1] Hancock and Gowing. *British War Economy*, page 52.

canned fish, canned fruit, dried fruit, canned peas and beans, condensed milk, cereal breakfast foods, biscuits, syrup, treacle, oat flakes and rolled oats, dried pulses, rice, sago and tapioca.

After the end of the war, as supplies improved, the number of points rationed foods was steadily reduced, and when eventually only eight were left in the system, it was abolished on 19 May 1950. Under the points rationing scheme, there was a greater freedom of choice than under straight rationing, and it also allowed an element of competition between traders, since there was no consumer registration. It was, however, administratively expensive, and a special consumer survey was necessary in order to regulate demand and supply. Points rationing in effect constitutes a supplementary form of currency by means of which the demand for, and supply of, a group of foods may be equated. The total points value of the coupons issued for use in a period must be equal to, or at least not more than, the total point value of the supplies available.

Chocolate and sugar confectionery was put into a special rationing scheme called the personal points scheme, so that each member of a household might have his or her own coupons which were available at any shop without registration. Rationing of chocolate and sugar confectionery was suspended for a short time after the war, but had to be re-imposed as the demand proved too great for the available supplies.

Yet another method of rationing was the scheme for controlled distribution for liquid milk and milk powder, shell eggs, dried eggs and oranges.

British and Continental Rationing Compared. The British system of rationing differed in many respects from that adopted in other countries. In Germany and the German-occupied area a rigid system of specific rationing was applied to almost all foods and this rigidity necessitated a high degree of differentiation as between different categories of consumer. Consumers were classified on the basis of occupation into normal consumers, night workers, heavy workers, very heavy workers and agricultural workers. Manual workers, in addition to extra meat, received substantial additions of bread and fats, graded so as to provide the extra calories required according to the severity of their work. Further differences in rations were made on the basis of age, sex and health. Children, nursing and expectant mothers and invalids received proportionally larger rations of protective foods, particularly milk.

In Britain during the war, bread, potatoes and vegetables were sufficiently plentiful to obviate the necessity of differential rationing as it was possible for the individual consumer to adapt the calories in the diet to requirements by consuming more of these commodities. Rationing in Britain was concerned mainly with the protein foods, milk and fats, and as need for these varies less as between adults, a uniform system of rationing was possible. A League of Nations Study of. War-time Rationing and Consumption in 1942 summed up the position in these words. "The most outstanding characteristic of the British system is its high degree of flexibility, as opposed to the rigidity of the German system. Its function is not to regiment the total level of consumption, which is largely determined by individual demand for the unrationed foods serving as budget regulators, but to secure to the whole population the elements necessary to a sound diet" (page 64).

It is probable that had Britain's food supplies fallen lower, a differential system of rationing would have been necessary and at one time after the war the system was being seriously considered. Extra meat for miners and the moving of greater supplies to mining areas was a first step in this direction. When bread rationing was introduced in 1946, some degree of differential rationing was found essential. The scale adopted is given in Table 27 of the Statistical Appendix.

Control over Distribution. Rationing at fixed prices necessitated control of the distributive trades. Imported supplies were distributed by war-time associations of traders, acting as agents of the Ministry of Food, and selling to licensed wholesalers who in turn sold to retailers registered with them. Home growers and home producers were required in general to dispose of their produce to the Ministry, or to buyers or first-hand distributors approved by the Ministry. Wheat and other cereals were collected and sent to controlled flour mills by authorized grain merchants. The Ministry of Food became the sole buyer of fat cattle, calves, sheep, lambs and pigs at specified collecting centres, and livestock could not be slaughtered without a special permit except in Government slaughter-houses or bacon factories. Eggs had to be brought to licensed Egg Packing Stations, where the price paid to the producer was higher than he could obtain legally by selling privately. Beet sugar was purchased from the British Sugar Corporation. Potatoes were controlled through the Potato Marketing Board and fish through allocation committees at the ports. There was little or no control over the distribution of fresh fruit and vegetables, poultry, rabbits and game, except as regards price. Successful control over distribution depended on the extent to which the flow of supplies could be directed through a few channels.

Licensing. Practically all firms manufacturing or distributing food were controlled by the Ministry of Food during the war by means of a licensing system. After the war ended, the licensing system was considerably relaxed, commencing with fresh fruit and vegetables and fish until by 1948 retail distributors (other than retailers of milk, butchers'-meat and chocolate and sugar confectionery) were freed from restrictions, control being maintained through buying permits or authorizations enabling traders to obtain the appropriate quantities of rationed or allocated foodstuffs.

Liquid Milk Distribution. Special interest attaches to the distribution of liquid milk in view of its importance to the health of children and their mothers. All milk was bought through the agency of the Milk Marketing Board, and the Ministry of Food enforced economies in retail distribution by limiting consumers to particular retailers in their district, or to the Co-operative Stores. Supplies were guaranteed to certain "priority classes" of consumer such as expectant mothers, young children, invalids and certain institutions. The rest of the community—the non-priority consumers—got what milk remained, amounting generally to two pints a head a week in the winter, and up to three or occasionally four pints a head a week in the summer. The distribution of milk was carefully regulated, the policy being to increase the direct consumption of milk, particularly by expectant and nursing mothers and by children. There was, therefore, far less milk available for processing and manufacturing purposes, and that only in the summer when supplies were plentiful. In pre-war years about one-third of the total milk production went to manufacture, including butter, cheese and condensed milk and various products such as cream, ice cream and milk chocolate. By the end of the war, the percentage going to manufacturing usages was only about 12 per cent. The manufacture of cream, ice cream and milk chocolate was prohibited, and that of butter was greatly reduced; such supplies of milk as were available for manufacture being used in the main for the production of cheese and condensed and dried milk.

During the first two years of the war, when farmers were converting their grasslands into arable, there was no marked rise in the production of milk sold off farms, and the increase in liquid milk consumption was secured by reducing the amount going to manufacturers. The total volume of milk produced did not regain the pre-war total of 1,780 million gallons until 1945, but milk sales off farms were increased by a reduction in the amounts consumed on the farms, including that fed to stock or used for making butter on the farm. Before the war, nearly one-third of the milk produced was consumed on farms, but during the war this was reduced to about 20 per cent. The farmers were faced with considerable difficulty in maintaining their supplies of milk as the feedingstuffs formerly imported practically disappeared.

Control of Imports. On the outbreak of the war, the Government requisitioned stocks of food in this country and also those stocks abroad which were under the control of British nationals. The Government also secured powers to control the importation of food, but at first these controls were of a somewhat patchwork nature and it was not until 1940 that the controls became really effective. The main aim was to secure that the best use would be made of the available shipping, and after March 1940, all food had to be imported either on direct Ministry of Food account or under licence. The Ministry of

Food itself became the sole importer of all the main foodstuffs, including cereals, oils and fats, meat, bacon, dairy products, sugar, starch, dried fruits, tea, coffee and cocoa. To procure supplies, buying agencies were established in all the main centres of the world, and many bulk contracts were negotiated with overseas governments or with organizations of overseas producers.

Storage and Transport of Foodstuffs. Where necessary the Ministry of Food arranges for the shipping, transport and storage of foodstuffs in conjunction with the Ministry of Transport. These activities include the chartering of ocean-going shipping through the Baltic Exchange Chartering Committee, unloading of cargoes at the ports, and the internal movement of food from the docks to warehouses, cold stores and first-hand distributors. The Ministry also controls or owns extensive warehousing and cold storage accommodation.

Control of Home-Produced Food. Home-produced food was also brought under the control of the Ministry of Food. The Agricultural Departments were responsible for encouraging the growing of food but the Ministry of Food was given the task of distributing the food after it had left the farm; the farm gate being taken as the dividing line between the responsibilities of the food and agricultural Ministries.

Price Control. Immediately on the outbreak of war, orders were made controlling the prices of all the main foodstuffs. For some foods such as flour and sugar, specific maximum prices were fixed, but for the majority there were "standstill" orders which prohibited prices higher than those for corresponding qualities during a given earlier period, generally the week ending 25 August 1939. These "standstill" orders were of a temporary nature and were gradually replaced by specific price orders when the necessary detailed investigations into prices had been made. The landed cost of many important imported foodstuffs soon increased owing to the inevitable rise in ocean freight rates, and these increases if passed on to the consumer would have been considerable and would have led to a marked rise in the cost of living index. As many wage agreements were tied to the cost of living index, this would have given impetus to a vicious spiral of inflation which at all costs it was felt necessary to avoid. It was therefore decided, in December 1939, to hold retail prices of food steady by means of subsidies from the Exchequer.

With most foods, where a subsidy is involved, the Ministry sells to first-hand distributors at prices lower than those paid for their purchase. Where the Ministry is not the owner of the commodity other methods are adopted. Payments, for example, are made to millers at a rate calculated to give them a fixed margin of profit on sales of flour at the controlled prices.

It was necessary to fix prices not only at the retail stage but at all stages of distribution. The principle adopted was that the trader at any stage in the distribution of food should be allowed a fair return, but no more, for the service he rendered. The practical application of the principle, however, was not easy, and at first profit margins were fixed by determining the gross profits earned before the war by representative firms in the particular branch of the trade concerned. Adjustments were then made for known wartime changes in costs. This procedure was beset with many difficulties; it was not easy in so diverse a trade as food distribution to find what were the "representative" firms especially as in practice the firms handled perhaps hundreds of varieties of food. Moreover, war-time movements of population might have reduced one trader's turnover drastically, but greatly increased that of another. The margins had to be such that they were sufficient to enable existing traders to remain in business, but this meant that in order to maintain the continuance of distribution, the margins had to err on the side of generosity. Periodic costing investigations, however, were introduced, with the object of reducing margins where they could be shown to be excessive. Price control by itself was not sufficient because the result would have been to increase the number of would-be purchasers, or to drive stocks "under the counter" for sale to favoured customers. There was also the difficulty that under a rigid price control system, the tendency would be for the goods to be sold near their place of origin so as to save transport costs. This was noticeable, for example, with home-grown fruit, rabbits and poultry when there was no advantage, indeed the contrary, in selling them outside the producing area. In the later stages of the war, the remedy adopted was to fix different maximum prices for different areas, so differentiated as to enable the trader to recoup any extra transport costs that might be involved. Another method was for the Ministry of Food, as in the case of fish, to pay all transport charges.

In general, however, control of prices was accompanied by rationing, points rationing or some form of controlled distribution. As the war progressed price control was extended, and at the beginning of 1941 some forty different types of food were controlled by specific price orders. By the end of that year the number of types of food specifically controlled had risen to about eighty. The last to be included were green vegetables, and this was not done until after 1943, because of the difficulty involved in defining such foods. How far, for example, should inedible matter such as stalks, useless outside leaves, or the like, be included in the weight? Because of these and similar difficulties the price orders for green vegetables were never fully satisfactory, despite the adoption of many ingenious definitions of trimming.

The proportion of household expenditure on food covered by price control rose steadily from 48 per cent in 1940 to 60 per cent in 1941, to 86 per cent in 1942, and to about 95 per cent from 1943 to the end of the war.[1]

Growth of Subsidies. As world supplies of food became scarcer and their prices rose, and as home agricultural prices increased as a result of rising costs of production, the amounts of subsidies required to stabilize retail prices rose, and it also became necessary to include foods previously unsubsidized such as milk products, sugar and eggs. The annual net cost of food subsidies borne by the Ministry of Food increased from £13 million in 1939–40 to £168 million in 1944–45. In Table 19 of the Statistical Appendix details of the distribution of these sums as between different foods are given, and in Tables 17

[1] *How Britain was Fed in War Time,* page 38.

and 18 the effect of subsidies in reducing the retail prices of different kinds of food will be seen.

In addition to the subsidies borne by the Ministry of Food, the Ministry of War Transport bore the excess cost of carrying imports to the United Kingdom, which resulted from the stabilization of ocean freight rates at a level insufficient to cover the full cost of war risk insurance. It is not possible to compute exactly the share which should be allocated against food imports, but in the later years of the war, this was estimated to have been about £5 million per annum. Other Government Departments bore the cost of subsidies on lime for farmers and of acreage payments on wheat, rye and potatoes to the extent of about £30 million annually. The acreage payments were not true subsidies, as they were taken into account in fixing the prices of these foodstuffs.

Why Rationing Continues. In most European countries, food rationing during the Second World War, and for some years thereafter, was more comprehensive and more sharply differentiated as between different groups in the population than it was in Britain or than it had been during the First World War. The British system was more flexible, largely because food supplies were somewhat larger, but it has been continued long after food rationing was dispensed with in other countries. The explanation of this continuance of food rationing for such a long period in peace time is no doubt to be found in several factors. Britain depends on food imports to a greater extent than do other countries, and the financing of food imports has presented difficulties. Two world wars seriously eroded British overseas investments, and this has meant that Britain's balance of payments has been adversely affected by the loss of interest payments from abroad. Exports practically ceased during the Second World War, and large debts were incurred overseas. The terms of trade have turned against this country because of a relative strengthening in the position of countries exporting food and raw materials as compared with those exporting manufactured goods. Food surpluses since the end of the Second World War have been largely concentrated in the hard currency countries and Britain has been short of dollars.

In addition to the repercussions of the international food situation and international financing, there have been also reactions on the food supplies position from the side of internal politics. Britain has had a long tradition of cheap imported food, and in pursuance of a policy of keeping down the cost of food, subsidies have risen to a dangerous height. Increase in rations, still more de-rationing, would automatically involve larger subsidies. Government policy has aimed at making equal amounts available to all at a price which all can pay, and this policy of egalitarianism has precluded resort to higher prices, or different prices for amounts beyond the ration.

Local Organization. Rationing and control of food distribution necessitates an elaborate local organization if efficiency is to be secured in the working of these controls, and if the convenience of the public is to be met. Local offices have to be provided so that all members of the public can call personally to obtain ration books, notify changes of address, obtain emergency food cards for use when away from home, and to make inquiries on rationing and other food matters. They have also to provide facilities for the issue of permits to traders for the purchase of supplies and for the issue of licences to retail traders and proprietors of catering establishments.

The organization had also to be tied up with arrangements for national defence so that local food supplies could be maintained in the event of heavy air raids cutting off communication with headquarters or of actual invasion. A two-tier system of control was therefore adopted, consisting of 19 Divisional Food Offices, which coincided with the Civil Defence Regions, and some 1,250 local food office areas based on local government areas. In each Division the Minister of Food was represented by a Divisional Food Officer responsible for the co-ordination of local administration in his Division, and acting as a link between the local food offices and Headquarters. Each Local Food Office was under the charge of a Food Executive Officer; usually in the early days of the war this official was the clerk to the local authority or one of his deputies. The Food Executive Officer also acts as secretary of the local Food Control Committee, consisting of representatives of traders, trade employees and consumers in the area. The functions of these committees is in general advisory but they also possess powers to investigate suspected offences against the food regulations, and to prosecute offenders. The organization was planned before the war broke out, and Local Authorities were asked to select their Food Executive Officer and provide key personnel to man the offices from among their staffs. The machinery was thus able to come into operation immediately on the outbreak of war, and as it was found to work successfully, very few changes were necessary during the war or after, though it has now been considerably simplified, and some economies have been made in man-power and offices. As long as any major foods remain rationed, however, local machinery for administration is required and extensive economies are not likely to be effected.[1]

---

[1] For more detailed information on the subject of this chapter the reader is referred to R. J. Hammond. *Food*, Volume I, *The Growth of Policy* in the "Official History of the War" series.

CHAPTER EIGHT

Government Purchasing of Food

THE war was responsible for great changes in the system of purchasing food from overseas. Formerly practically all food was obtained through private channels and was financed through the ordinary machinery of international trade. World-famed markets were established in London or the provinces through which vast quantities of food passed for consumption in this country and which also carried on an extensive entrepôt trade. The Baltic Exchange, Mincing Lane, the London Commercial Sale Rooms, the General Produce Brokers' Association of London and many specialized associations concerned with commodities such as tea, coffee, cocoa, sugar or copra helped to make London the centre of the world's trade in food. The commissions, brokerages and payments for financial services, which were earned in connection with the food import and re-export trades, made an important contribution to Britain's invisible exports.

On the outbreak of war, the Ministry of Food, as explained in Chapter Seven, became the sole importer of all the main foodstuffs, and the various commodity exchanges were closed down. The arrangements made during the war have been continued in peace time, and the Ministry remains responsible for the purchase of all the more important foods including cereals, animal feedingstuffs, meat, sugar, dairy produce, coffee and cocoa. A full list of the foodstuffs imported on Government account is given below, which sets out the position as it was in the summer of 1950.

Other foodstuffs which are of less importance can be imported by private traders under a licensing system. There are two types of licence, the individual specific licence which involves a trader in obtaining a licence for any particular import of the food concerned which he may desire to make

Foodstuffs imported on Government Account, as at June 1950

The following is a list of foodstuffs of which the Government was the sole importer.

Cereals and Animal Feedingstuffs

Wheat	Dun Peas
Flour	Locust Beans
Rye	Cassava Root
Maize	Oilcake and Meal
Barley	Fish Meal
Oats	Bone Meal
Wheat Offals	Meat Meal
Rice Bran	Whalemeat Meal
Maple Peas	

Oils and Oilseeds

Benniseed	Linseed
Copra	Linseed Oil
Cotton Seed	Maize Oil
Cottonseed Oil	Palm Kernels
Groundnuts	Palm Kernel Oil
Groundnut Oil	Palm Oil
Coconut Oil	Sunflower Seed
Kapok Seed	Sunflowerseed Oil
Illipe Nuts	Soya Beans
Shea Nuts	Niger Seed

Animal Fats

Lard	Tallow
Premier Jus	Dripping

Marine Oils

Whale Oil	Vitamin "A" Oil
Herring Oil	(some)
Other Fish Oil	

Sugar

Medicinal Glucose

Rice

Starch and Starch Products

Farine	Maize Starch
Farina	Cassava Starch
Dextrine	Tapioca

Meat

Carcase Meat and Offals
Canned Corned Meat

Bacon and Ham

Canned Fish

Barracouta	Pilchards
Sardines	Crabs
Tunny	Crawfish
Brisling	Salmon
Sild	

Milk Products

Cheese (ration and some fancy cheeses)	Block Milk
	Milk Powder (some)
Butter	Buttermilk
Condensed Milk	Whey Powder

Eggs and Egg Products

Eggs in shell (hen and duck)	Dried Albumen
	Dried Yolk
Frozen Eggs	Glycerine Yolk
Dried Egg	

Dried Fruit

Currants	Prunes
Sultanas	Raisins
Apricots	Dates
Pears	

Fresh Fruit and Vegetables

Apples	Potatoes (ware)
Bananas	

Canned Fruit

Peaches	Two Fruits
Pears	Fruit Cocktail
Apricots	Grapes
Pineapples	Mandarin Oranges
Grapefruit	

Orange Juice (Welfare)

Tea (except China Tea)

Raw Coffee

Cocoa

Poultry and *rabbits* were also being bought on Government account but were due to revert to private trade.

and the open general licence under which importers may bring in what they wish of the commodities coming under this system. Frequently, however, there has been an upper limit placed on the total amount of a commodity which can be imported under open general licence, for example, imports may be allowed freely up to a pre-determined amount of currency. In May 1950, the Minister of Food said in the House of Commons that food importations on private account then amounted to about one-fifth in value of total food imports. By that date more than 300 items of food had been handed back to private trade, including many commodities such as onions, cheeses, canned tomatoes, tomato purée, lemons, oranges, grape-fruit and fruit pulp, which previously had been imported on government account. The field of private importations of foodstuffs had also been enlarged by discontinuing or relaxing controls by licensing. Many foods had been transferred to open general licences, whereby they could be freely imported from all countries with which Britain had no balance of payments problem. Liberalization of European trade had also greatly widened the field of private trade in food.

The procurement of food in Britain since the war has been based on import planning. This has involved elaborate programming, and has been carried into effect mainly through the Government's bulk purchases and long-term contracts, supplemented in the case of less important commodities by private buying abroad. Currency has been the limiting factor in the procurement of food supplies in recent years, and this has been reflected in the programming procedure. Each year a programme for food imports has been drawn up fixing a total budget for expenditure on these food imports. Within this total, amounts are then allocated to each of the main foods.

State-trading. During the war, control of shipping and foreign exchange together with the necessity for strict regulation of food distribution led the Government to purchase practically all kinds of food to the exclusion of private traders from primary markets. The term state-trading is used to describe government monopoly buying in its most general sense. The actual methods adopted vary considerably since the Government may deal directly with other governments, as is the case with the purchase of meat from the Argentine; it may deal through agencies with a multiplicity of small traders in various countries or it may place its contracts with organizations of producers.

Government monopoly buying does not necessarily mean bulk purchasing, though in the case of the staple commodities such as grain and meat, bulk purchase has been fairly general. This has led to some confusion between state-trading and bulk purchase, as it is often thought that the two are synonymous. Bulk purchase does not necessarily mean long-term contracts though here again in practice many bulk purchase contracts have been long-term contracts such as the Canadian Wheat Agreement which covered four years. Considerable variations have occurred in long-term contracts. Sometimes the price has been fixed for the duration of the contract, or at least fixed within limits, though in many contracts there have been review clauses, or even arrangements for annual price reviews. In 1949, the Government was committed to 54 long-term contracts of which 12 related to milk products and eggs, 12 to oils and fats, 8 to meat and bacon and 7 to sugar. Of these 54 contracts, 24 were with British Colonies, 6 with Australia and 4 each with Canada and New Zealand.

Much political controversy has centred around the question of state-trading in food and in particular bulk purchasing has been stoutly upheld by some and as strongly attacked by others. During the war, there was little or no difference of opinion about the inevitable necessity of state-trading, but since then controversy has been acute.[1] It is not easy to summarize the various arguments which have been advanced on both sides, as the matter has become obscured by party polemics and prejudices. Briefly, however, the case for state purchase rests largely on the assumption that when the Government guarantee a ration of so much a week to the

[1] See for example the Report of the Debate in the House of Commons on Food Imports (Private Trading) in Hansard, 12 May 1950. Vol. 475, No. 46.

consumer, it cannot disinterest itself in the procurement of supplies sufficient to honour that ration. It is argued that planning of food supplies is not possible without bulk buying, and that in any case we must buy in bulk because other countries insist on selling in bulk. In connection with planning, it is also argued that we can only maintain our system of guaranteed prices and guaranteed markets to our own farming community if the Government has control over the imports of food. Government purchase, it is also claimed, facilitates the allocation of resources according to a pattern dictated by balance of payments considerations, and these, it is stressed, have been the limiting factors during recent years in our ability to secure many kinds of food.

Bulk Buying. The main argument used in favour of bulk buying (i.e., buying in large lots greater than the normal market transactions usual for the particular type of commodity) is essentially that of monopoly purchase. Competition among buyers is eliminated and it is contended, therefore, that more favourable prices can be obtained. Where the seller is a monopolist, as in countries where the State controls the sale of all supplies of a particular foodstuff and where these are an important part of the total world exportable surplus, it is argued that only the government can bargain adequately for bulk supplies. The large monopoly buyer can offer solid advantages to the larger sellers since he can eliminate for them the risk of a fall in world price below the bulk purchase price so far as the quantity covered by the bulk purchase is concerned. The bulk buyer can save sellers the extra cost of many small sales.

Long-term contracts. If long-term contracts are negotiated, the buyer can offer an assured market for a term of years, and this is often regarded by producers as an important advantage, enabling growers to plan ahead with security. On a rising market, the ability to offer long-term contracts for large quantities affords a bulk buyer favourable opportunities to buy at prices below the average which would have ruled over the period, had he continued to buy in small parcels. In support of the contention that long-term contracts have great advantages in such circumstances, the experience of the Canadian Wheat Agreement is often quoted, as, during the four years' period of the Agreement, Britain was able to secure wheat below the price ruling in the world markets.

Case against State-trading. Those who oppose state-trading in principle, argue that it tends to mix diplomacy with business deals, and that negotiations are inevitably hampered by extraneous political considerations, indiscreet promises or intemperate comments. It is also contended that government buyers may not have as much experience as trade buyers, and the senior civil servants to whom they are responsible may have no commercial experience of any kind and may be over-cautious at the wrong time. Moreover, the senior civil servants ultimately responsible for high level decisions are frequently changed, since in theory the individual is deemed capable of undertaking any responsibility at his particular level, and specialization has not been encouraged as it would be in business undertakings. It is true that when the system of trade buying was introduced during the war, the negotiators were assisted by experts from private trade who had had long experience, and were equipped with great technical knowledge of the commodities concerned, but as time goes on and state-trading remains a monopoly, the field from which technical knowledge can be drawn grows smaller and smaller. The private trader, it is argued, who himself bears the risks of his enterprise, is on the whole a better negotiator than the government negotiator. He establishes good will in commercial circles, and is well-known to his opposite numbers in the foreign country, whereas government officials appear to be frequently changed. The trader goes about his business quietly, whereas the dispatch of a mission or a party of government negotiators is heralded so to speak with a fanfare of trumpets, and if results favourable to the particular country are not obtained, considerable ill-will may result. Probably one of the most serious limitations is that large-scale bulk buying does not allow mistakes being made because a mistake if made is likely to be a gigantic one. In commerce, it is a truism that a buyer cannot always be right, and he cannot help on occasion making a "bad buy". Where the amounts involved in a particular transaction are small, this is nothing like so serious as where they are large. Where there is a multiplicity of buyers, it is possible for tentative buying to start on a small scale, and pave the way for larger dealings. The single buyer may not be well enough informed and technically knowledgeable about the numerous varieties and qualities which are to be found where some commodities are concerned, and may not know, therefore, the right amount to buy of each at its appropriate price. Where there are many buyers, they can specialize in meeting the needs of particular users. A case in point is tea, where there are many varieties and the advantages of bulk buying are outweighed by the need for specialization. State purchasing, it is also said, tends to overlook alternative, though minor sources of supply, which might be appreciable in the aggregate, whereas the small trader can deal economically in such small lots. Much discussion has centred during recent years on the question of the quality of the produce obtained through bulk buying. It is asserted that inevitably quality will suffer because the large buyer gets the average or even low quality produce since he cannot demand that all should be of the best quality, for the simple reason that not enough would be available, and as state buying has not favoured differential prices for better qualities, the choicer qualities naturally go to the private buyers coming from other countries which have now given up bulk buying by the State. Before the war, Britain was the centre of the world market in food and her position as an international trading centre brought a considerable income from invisible exports, including profits from trade, insurance, banking, chartering and other facilities provided by this country. Continuation of state-trading so long after the end of the war has prevented Britain from regaining her position as a world market, and has meant the loss of an important contribution to invisible exports. To sum up the position as the writer sees it, it is obvious that it is easier to introduce state-trading and state control of imports, than it is to discard the apparatus of state-trading once it has been established. Government buying, however, is not essential, as is sometimes asserted, to the smooth working of the rationing and food subsidies schemes. There do not seem to be any insuperable difficulties connected with these matters which would prevent a return to private buying as the organization of the tea trade has shown. Neither is it essential to have state-trading in order to control the amount of imports coming into the country. If necessary, it would be a comparatively simple matter to set a maximum to the amounts which could be imported by private traders.

During the war, there was a good case for state-trading and possibly also for some years thereafter it could be argued that the unsettled state of the world, the food shortages and Britain's procurement responsibilities made it undesirable to disturb the system which had grown up. Also during this period, prices were rising, and this made long-term bulk contracts more attractive. As the years passed and the special considerations which applied during the war came to be less and less applicable, the case for reversion to private trading became stronger. There has in fact been a partial, though slow, return to private trading, and this was gathering momentum until the necessity for stock-piling acted as a brake on further progress in this direction. It does not follow, however, that because some stockpiling is necessary, state-trading must be retained over the whole field. On balance, the weight of argument seems to favour the case against bulk purchase by governments. Inevitably, what should be ordinary commercial transactions take on the aspect of political negotiations, and are apt to cause bad feelings between nations. There also appears to be special cogency in the argument that Britain used to gain much from her position as the centre of world trade in foodstuffs and the advantages which are to be gained from these invisible exports should not be lightly foregone. Further, it has been argued, experience with the Argentine has shown that a state monopoly buyer is not able to-day to exert any more influence than could be exerted by traders in the ordinary course of trade, because questions of politics, prestige and extraneous factors become involved when government-to-government bargains are involved.

Finally, it is hard to believe that the necessarily cumbrous procedure of state-trading is well suited to the highly technical and diversified problems which are involved in purchasing on the world's food markets.

CHAPTER NINE

Communal Feeding

OVER the past ten years there has been a great increase in the habit of eating outside the home in works canteens, restaurants and other catering establishments. This development has been due to a number of causes ranging from full employment and higher wages to lack of domestic help in the home. The main cause, however, was food shortages, and the fact that food coupons did not have to be surrendered for meals eaten in catering establishments. During the war, when the habit of eating out became established on a wider basis than formerly, the demand for hot meals away from home was reinforced by such factors as the transference of labour, the conscription of women, the dispersal of factories and shortage of suitable food for making sandwiches.

In Britain, with some minor exceptions, there was no system of differential rations for workers based on the nature of the employment, such as was adopted by most other countries engaged in the war. The main exceptions to the system of equal rations for all were based on the nutritional needs of groups such as children and nursing and expectant mothers who required greater amounts of proteins, or other nutrients. Industrial workers and in particular those engaged on heavy work were provided with the extra food they needed by the introduction of works canteens which over a large field of industry were made obligatory on firms, and by the allocation of extra supplies to this type of catering establishment. Agricultural workers and miners, for whom canteens were not usually available, were given extra rations of cheese, and miners, since the war, have been granted extra meat. Seamen were placed in a special ration category, since they were entirely dependent on their rations while at sea, and in any case were engaged in a hard and hazardous occupation, being in constant danger from the enemy and from the elements. The special scales have been continued since the war, as they are based on the standard of feeding laid down in the Merchant Shipping Acts. Fishermen normally at sea for more than a week at a time are allowed the same scale of rations as seamen. Other types of fishermen (except inshore fishermen) receive modified allowances. A policy of free access to catering establishments for all was maintained, though the ordinary catering establishments had smaller allocations of rationed foods than the industrial canteens. In the original plans for rationing it was intended that coupons should be surrendered in catering establishments for meals which included meat or bacon dishes, but when bacon was rationed, it was decided at the last moment not to demand coupons for meals. Thereafter, it came to be accepted as a set policy that occasional meals eaten-out in catering establishments should be regarded as additional to the domestic ration, as most of these meals would be eaten, in any case, by workers of various kinds, manual or non-manual, who could not return home for all their meals, and for whom canteens or staff dining-rooms were not available.

Residents at hotels and boarding houses staying longer than a few days, usually four days was taken as the dividing line, had to surrender their ration books. The supply of rationed foodstuffs was carefully regulated, and the efficiency with which the rationing scheme was administered prevented any marked abuse. Retribution usually followed quickly on any evasions, and this acted as a salutary deterrent on any who were tempted to deal on a "black market". The allocation of food to canteens, restaurants, tea shops, public houses and other catering establishments was on the basis of the number of "meals" and "hot beverages" served in a preceding period. This necessitated the careful recording of all meals and hot drinks served over the rationing period, and the careful scrutiny of the records at the local food offices. The amount of rationed foods was scaled so as to put the caterer on roughly the same basis as the housewife who had to spread her rations over a given number of meals a week. It was assumed for example that meat would be eaten at only two main meals each day, and therefore a meat ration of 1s. 2d. worth would, on the assumption made, entitle the caterer to one-fourteenth of this amount for each "main meal" served, that is one-pennyworth. The caterer, however, was given a free hand in allocating this amount to the individual customers. If some of the main meals served did not contain meat, he could serve more than the pennyworth with other meals so long as he did not exceed his allocation. Further, the more meals he served, the more rationed food he was allocated. Special provisions were also made for caterers to receive a proportionate amount of foods rationed under the points system, and systems of con-trolled distribution.

For the industrial canteens, the allowances were more generous, and larger amounts of meat, fats and sugar were granted than to ordinary catering establishments. The basis of the allocations was, however, essentially the same, apart from the differences in amounts.

Industrial Canteens. During the First World War, the pro-vision of works canteens received a considerable impetus. Before 1914, there were barely a hundred regular factory canteens, whereas by 1918 there were probably almost a thousand such canteens operating or in process of construction. After 1918, the numbers fell off greatly, and both managers and workers became apathetic. Even where canteens were provided, many of them were in fact only mess-rooms where workers could eat food they had brought from home and where simple facilities might be provided for heating that food. Since 1939, the mess rooms where they existed have given place to more fully equipped canteens. To-day, as was pointed out in a recent Report of the Chief Inspector of Factories, plans for new factories almost invariably include a canteen, suggesting that employers are coming to regard it as essential to provide a hot meal at the factory. It is also significant that in many advertisements for employees, one of the advantages stressed of employment with the firm is the provision of a can-teen serving good and cheap meals.

During the war, the canteen movement in industry received

a great impetus, and as early as 1940, the Ministry of Labour and National Service was empowered to require the establishment of a canteen at any factory employing more than 250 persons engaged on the production of munitions or on other work on behalf of the Crown. In 1943, the limitation regarding the type of work was abolished, and the regulation applied to any factory employing more than 250 persons. Compulsory provisions were also made for setting up canteens at the docks, on building sites and at collieries. As a result of legislation the number of canteens increased greatly among the larger firms, but what was more significant was the remarkable increase in the number of canteens provided by firms employing less than 250 persons in their factories and without any legal obligation to make such provisions for the feeding of their workers. By the end of 1941, 2,530 factories, each employing under 250 persons, were providing canteens for their workers. Three years later the number had increased to 6,584. In the same period, the total number of canteens in factories of all sizes increased from 5,695 to 11,630. The number of canteens provided at building sites was 787 in 1941 and 868 in 1942, but the number of these declined thereafter, and fell to 179 in 1945, owing to the reduction in the building programme. The number of canteens at docks which was 110 in 1941 had risen steadily through slowly during the war and was 180 in 1945. (See Table 23 in the Statistical Appendix.)

Summing up the position in 1942, Lord Woolton stated that by then "great strides had been made in the task of feeding the worker at his work, and a great industrial revolution has taken place. Permanent progress has been made in industrial outlook and practice, and when peace comes, we must not go back on this standard which has been established under stress of war."

Many difficulties had to be surmounted before canteens could be provided. In the first place, there were the difficulties associated with building, or the adaptation of existing premises at a time when labour was scarce and when there were also shortages of the necessary equipment, though this was partially overcome by granting priorities to industrial canteens.

During the early years of the war, workers were somewhat apathetic towards the canteens which were being provided, but attitudes changed as the food shortages got more stringent. There were also great difficulties in obtaining the necessary skilled personnel to manage and operate the canteens. To help with these problems the Chief Inspector of Factories appointed a number of Factory Canteen Advisers who had special knowledge of catering, nutrition and domestic science to advise employers and canteen managers and manageresses about the many problems connected with large-scale feeding. These advisers were available to every firm for help and advice on such matters as layout, equipment, staffing, cooking, menu planning and service. To train the large number of managers and manageresses required to staff the new canteens, special training courses, both full-time and part-time, were initiated by the Department of Industrial Administration at the Manchester College of Technology, and were later extended to other parts of the country. During and since the war, despite all the difficulties associated with the supply of the requisite materials, which became even scarcer as the war progressed, there has been a great development in the attractiveness of factory canteens. In particular, colour has been effectively used to improve the appearance of many canteens, and it would not be going too far to say that the developments in this direction have been almost revolutionary. There has also been a notable improvement in the eating habits and table manners of factory workers, as will be borne out by anyone who can remember back to conditions in the First World War. This is a social development of considerable significance, which, though seldom commented upon, is part of a general improvement in standards of living and conduct, which is helping to make social distinctions less harsh and rigid.

Not a few firms have made special efforts to provide suitably balanced meals at reduced prices for the juvenile workers. Commenting on this development, the Chief Inspector of Factories in his Annual Report for the year 1944 stated that: "It is apparent that the attitude of most firms is favourable in principle to giving some special service to young persons, but that some measure of persuasion is needed to develop this into positive interest. The proper feeding of the young is a service to the community of the future which those at the head of affairs to-day have it in their power to give, and it should be treated accordingly. This service can only be effectively rendered if the provision of the food (whether at a cheaper rate or not) is accompanied by educative effort and by accurate observation of results."[1]

Since the war, industrial canteens, instead of diminishing rapidly in number as they did after the First World War, have continued to increase, and it is noteworthy that the increase has been especially rapid in the smaller factories. Full employment and higher wages have made it possible for workers to patronize the canteens, and canteen prices have been very moderate owing to the financial help which is given to them by so many firms in the form of rent-free premises, provision of services such as heating and lighting, or even sometimes direct subsidy to the costs of administration and running. In actual fact, few industrial canteens pay their way in the full commercial sense. The continuance of food rationing has of course been a powerful influence in the continued progress of the industrial canteen movement, as the canteens provide a welcome addition to scarce rationed foods such as meat.

No adequate solution has yet been found to the problem of providing facilities for hot meals at building sites. On small sites, the difficulties are obvious, but even on larger sites the men may be employed by numerous contractors, none of whom employs a sufficient number to justify a canteen. Mobile canteens have been tried, but these are very expensive if the sites are dispersed over a large area. A packed meals service has had better results, but it does not provide for a hot meal which is so much to be preferred to sandwiches or cold snacks.

Provision of Hot Drinks and Milk. Industrial workers where canteen facilities are not available can obtain supplies of tea, milk and sugar, so that hot beverages can be brewed commun-

[1] Cmd. 6698.

ally during working hours. Office workers are allowed half quantities of tea and milk, but no sugar. In certain occupations where the conditions of work prevent arrangements being made for communal brewing of tea, employers are given supplies of tea, milk and sugar for issue in "dry" form for individual brewing by employees. Among workers covered by this arrangement are certain classes of railwaymen, country roadmen and canal workers.

Certain classes of industrial workers such as blast-furnace-men, tinplate workers and salt workers, who because of the temperatures in which they work, or because of other reasons, need to drink an exceptional amount of liquid are allowed a higher scale.

Priority supplies of milk not exceeding one pint a worker a day are available for consumption as a beverage during working hours to the operatives in certain undertakings in which milk is desirable on medical grounds.

In order that young workers may obtain additional first-class protein, National Milk Cocoa has been made available to all workers under 21 years of age in factories, businesses and agriculture, and to all youth organizations and students not benefiting under the Milk-in-Schools Scheme.

British Restaurants. In 1940, Local Authorities were encouraged by the Ministry of Food to set up communal feeding centres as a means of providing cheap but nourishing meals for those people who were obliged to eat away from home and who were not able to avail themselves of the services of a canteen. Financial assistance was provided by the central government to local authorities on a repayment basis to cover capital expenditure. The prices charged are required to cover all the costs, including a statutory charge for administrative services provided by the Town Hall staffs. No special privileges have been granted as regards the allocation of rationed foodstuffs, but they proved useful in supplementing catering facilities in areas where these were short, and in some areas, small firms utilized the local British Restaurant to obtain cooked food, which was brought to the factory in insulated containers. Generally, British Restaurants were organized on the cafeteria or self-service system, thus providing a quick service and keeping down wages costs. By the end of 1943, there were 2,119 British Restaurants in operation, serving 619,000 meals daily, but this was the high-water mark, and the number dropped considerably in the following years until 1947, when British Restaurants as they were known during the war ceased to function. They did not completely disappear, however, as under the Civic Restaurants Act, 1947, local authorities were empowered to continue the provision of restaurants and the Ministry of Food invited them to take over the Ministry's assets in British Restaurants on repayment terms. Some 300 local authorities took advantage of the powers given them by this Act, though some 465 Authorities closed down their undertakings. The number of Civic Restaurants fell from 1,176 in 1947 to 678 in 1949, though some of this fall represents concentration of their restaurants on the part of certain local authorities. In an article on "The Finance of Civic Restaurants", G. Sugden, Borough Treasurer of West Bromwich, concludes after a detailed examination of accounts and statistics, that "success seems to lie mainly in controlling expenditure upon provisions and salaries and wages without damaging demand . . . the percentages which these items bear to income are really indices of management. They will reflect waste, unimaginative catering, overlapping or under-working and so on. And it is really upon efficient management that the success of the catering department will depend."[1]

Agricultural Workers. The feeding of agricultural workers has been a problem of peculiar difficulty since rationing was introduced. Suitable "spreads" or fillings for sandwiches were hard to obtain owing to shortages of these kinds of food. Agricultural workers have no canteens or British Restaurants to serve them as have their opposite numbers in the towns, and a "Rural Pie Scheme" was therefore introduced in 1942 to provide agricultural workers with meat pies, sandwiches and snacks. The food which was prepared by local bakers or by British Restaurants was distributed by voluntary organizations. The coverage of the scheme could never hope to be

[1] *Local Government Finance.* Oct. 1949.

8

complete, but, by 1942, it was serving some 5,000 villages and distributing some 1¼ million pies or other snacks weekly.

A special cheese ration was introduced for agricultural workers in May 1941, which was first at a rate of 8 oz., but was raised to 12 oz. at the end of that year. It remained at this level except during the second half of 1942, when it was temporarily 16 oz. The special cheese ration was extended later to certain other specified classes of workers, such as underground miners, road workers and quarry men.

During periods of seasonal activity such as hay-making, harvesting or lambing which involve working long hours in the field, farmers can obtain extra tea and sugar for their workers sufficient to provide four hot beverages a worker daily, and if there is no packed meal service available, they also get supplies sufficient to provide each worker with two snack meals a day.

Road Transport Workers. The road transport worker is in general faced with special difficulties in obtaining meals. The bus driver and conductor usually work a straight eight-hour shift, and the provision of meals is a serious problem. In many cities, therefore, the undertakings provide canteens at the depots or bus stations and some, such as Manchester Corporation and the London Transport Executive, have put mobile canteens into service, usually consisting of a converted single deck bus.

The long-distance lorry driver and his mate are in a more unfavourable position, and they have to rely on roadside cafés to obtain rest and refreshment. The roadside café catering for the lorry drivers has now become an institution in this country, and many hundreds of them are to be found up and down the main roads. Usually the atmosphere is personal and intimate, and the proprietor is known to all as "Charlie" or "Jack" or "Joe", but as regards amenities they are frequently much below the minimum standard which might rightly be expected by their users. Only too often the whole atmosphere is shoddy, as was emphasized in a pamphlet entitled *Road Transport Cafés*, published by the British Road Federation in 1948. "There is no exaggeration," this pamphlet states, "in claiming that all too few of the existing transport cafés cater conscientiously for the drivers' needs. Generally speaking, the café consists of no more than a single bare room, which may be large or small according to the size of the premises, furnished with plain wooden benches or kitchen chairs and cluttered tables with either no covering or with soiled and usually tattered oil-cloth." During the war, something was done to provide better meals for transport drivers by placing the roadside cafés serving them on the same basis for rationed foodstuffs as the industrial canteens, and their staffs were given special consideration when workers were being directed to war jobs.

Feeding of School Children. During the war, there was a considerable expansion in the school meals service, the million mark being exceeded in early 1943, as compared with a total of 160,000 in 1938-39. Expansion in the service continued steadily after the end of the war, and the number of school meals served in 1948 was over 2½ million. Expansion of the school meals scheme during the war was intended to make good any deficiencies in the children's diet which might have resulted from evacuation or the absence of mothers on war work. The main aim, however, was to secure that the children should obtain an adequate supply of certain foods, especially animal protein, which are essential to their growth and health. For this reason generous allocations were made, including twopennyworth of meat a main meal as compared with the pennyworth of the ordinary catering establishment. The value of the school meal service was amply proved during the war, and it has now been further extended so that over half the total number of children in attendance at day-schools are provided with a meal at school. The expansion would no doubt have been even greater but for limitations placed by shortage of equipment and lack of the necessary buildings.

The supply of milk to school children has also been greatly extended. Whereas in 1938-39 some 2½ million children were receiving supplies of milk at school, the number in 1948 was well over 4½ million, or nearly 88 per cent of those in attendance. The milk is normally supplied to the schools in one-third pint bottles with drinking straws. Before the war the Milk-in-Schools Scheme applied only to elementary schools, but during the war, it was extended to a wide range of schools, the amount of milk provided for each child being ⅓ pint. (See Tables 24 and 25 in the Statistical Appendix.)

Commercial Catering. The fact that meals could be obtained "off the ration" in commercial catering establishments such as hotels, restaurants, cafés, tea shops and the like, led to a considerable increase in the habit of eating-out. Though the number of meals taken increased during the war years, the actual number of undertakings declined somewhat, no doubt owing to shortage of labour. After the war, when conditions became easier, and licences could be more readily obtained, the number of establishments increased. In 1951 there were about 114,500 catering establishments open to the general public, and between them they served nearly 39 million "substantial" meals each week, compared with 24 million in industrial canteens and staff dining-rooms, and 40 million meals in establishments of the institutional type, and in day and nursery schools. The proportion of the nation's rationed food going to the commercial catering establishments, however, has never been very large, amounting only to about 3 per cent of the total.

Food Hygiene. Food poisoning cases have shown a steady increase during recent years, though in relation to the number of meals consumed in catering establishments, the number is fairly small. It is obvious that higher standards of food hygiene in this country are necessary, and it would seem that we have fallen behind what is being achieved in other countries, especially the United States and the Scandinavian countries. Food hygiene is now more important than it used to be for several reasons. More and more people are coming to live in the towns, and fewer people eat food that they have prepared themselves. Obviously the more hands the food passes through, the more are the opportunities for contamination. Careless handling of food in catering establishments may affect many persons, and there is also a danger in that such food may have been cooked many hours before it is eaten.

Public opinion is now coming to recognize the importance of clean food, and the dangers which may arise from careless handling in markets, shops and catering establishments. The matter has recently been considered by the Catering Trade Working Party, which in a Report on Hygiene in Catering Establishments, issued early in 1951, has recommended the registration by local authorities of all catering establishments, and their observation of a standard code for cleanliness. The Report urges that considerable improvement in hygienic conditions in catering establishments could be obtained by the adoption of codes of practice. Two codes are suggested, a standard code covering the essential requirements for clean food only, and a target code setting out what is considered necessary for securing that food served in catering establishments is prepared under the best possible conditions. The standard code which it is suggested should be obligatory sets out a number of requirements for limiting the infection of food from food handlers, and securing that the working premises are clean, adequately lit and hygienic. The Report states that while the conditions in many catering establishments are good, or at least satisfactory, there is also a considerable number of establishments in which unhygienic practices are only too common.

Practical steps to improve conditions of food handling have taken a number of forms. Thus the St. John Ambulance Association, following a successful experiment in Southport, has launched a national campaign for the institution of lectures on food hygiene suitable for those who handle food as part of their work. Certificates are to be granted to those who attain the requisite standard in an examination somewhat in the same way as First Aid Certificates have been granted for so many years by the Association.

Local Authorities are now becoming conscious of the importance of food hygiene, and by the beginning of 1951, some 30 local authorities had set up "Clean Food Guilds" or similar bodies in their areas, with the objective of securing higher standards of food handling in shops and catering establishments.

A useful and highly practical manual has been prepared by Marks & Spencer Ltd., entitled *Hygienic Food Handling*, under the general editorship of Dr. A. Lerner, as a guide for the firm's staff, though it has now been given a wider circulation. This points out the various factors which are involved in securing clean food handling, none of which it is stressed may be neglected without seriously lowering the standard. These factors are each discussed in detail with practical advice as to how the best standards may be maintained. Summarized, the factors involved are first, personal cleanliness of the persons handling the food, second, the care and attention necessary in regard to the foodstuffs themselves, third, service hygiene, fourth, the kind of equipment necessary and its proper cleaning and maintenance, fifth, care and cleanliness of the premises themselves and sixth, vermin control.

College of Food Technology. In order to provide the different sections of the food industry with training at a high level, a National College of Food Technology has been established in London. The courses provided cover the handling, preservation, and processing of meat, fish and other foods, together with their various derivatives and by-products. It is also intended that the courses should include instruction in those branches of science most closely concerned with changes which take place in food during preservation and processing. The courses are intended for mature students with a good foundation of science and with industrial experience.

Food Hygiene Legislation. Legislation to protect the consumer from inferior or adulterated foods and to secure better standards of food hygiene is contained in the Food and Drugs Act, 1938, and the Food and Drugs (Milk and Dairies) Act, 1944. Under the former Act, following an Order made in 1948 for the transfer of functions, the Minister of Food can make regulations regarding the advertising, labelling and composition of food, and has become responsible for food inspection and food hygiene generally. On taking over these functions, the Minister of Food stated in the House of Commons (21 July 1948) that it was his intention "to seek the co-operation of local authorities and their officers, the food trade and the public in a concerted effort to combat the dangers to health which result from the preparation, storage or handling of food in unclean or otherwise unsatisfactory conditions".

CHAPTER TEN

Food Supplies and Consumption
since the War

On the termination of hostilities, the general public believed that after a short period of readjustment, food shortages would quickly disappear as they had done after the First World War. In the event, these hopes of "jam to-morrow" were not to be realized, and the disappointment was the greater because during the war, shortages and privations had been borne on the whole cheerfully enough as part of the price which had to be paid for national survival and in the belief that they were only temporary hardships which would be relieved as soon as victory was achieved.

Surprise is often expressed that recovery should be so slow after the Second World War, especially as after the First World War agricultural production and world trade in food made a rapid recovery. Conditions, however, have been very different. The Second World War lasted longer, the extent of the damage done was much greater and the Japanese occupation of so much of South-East Asia disrupted agricultural production there to an enormous extent and threw the whole economy of South-East Asia out of balance. The world's population has increased since 1938, especially in Asia, and the increased demand for food has absorbed much of the improvements in agricultural methods which have so far been achieved. Britain has been in a position of peculiar difficulty, because she is so dependent on world trade in food. Other countries are attempting to raise their own standards of food consumption, and have been developing industries of their own. The terms of trade between the agricultural countries and the industrialized countries have changed, and now more exports have to be given by Britain in exchange for a fixed amount of food as compared with pre-war days.

World Food Shortage. Soon after the war, the world was faced with an acute shortage of food. Shortages in fats, meat, dairy products and sugar had been foreseen as shortages in these commodities had developed during the war, but quite unexpected was a serious shortage in grain supplies which meant that it would be no longer possible to make up for the deficiencies in other foods by increased consumption of cereals. The cause of the crisis was an exceptional succession of droughts in many of the world's main producing areas during 1945 and 1946, added to the war dislocation of agricultural production. In Continental Europe, the grain and potato harvests, especially in the Mediterranean region, were seriously affected by a drought in the summer of 1945; in French North Africa in the spring of that year the bread grain harvest was reduced to less than a third of the normal figure; in the Union of South Africa, wheat production was nearly halved; in New Zealand, butter production was seriously affected, and in India there was a general failure of the rains with a resultant serious reduction in grain crops.

Over Continental Europe as a whole, excluding U.S.S.R., the 1945 harvest of wheat and rye was only 31 million tons compared with 46 million tons a year earlier, and a pre-war average of 59 million tons. In the East, there was an equally serious fall in rice production, the two principal rice-exporting countries, namely Burma and Thailand, producing slightly under 5 million tons in 1946, as against a pre-war average of nearly 8½ million tons.

In a White Paper[1] on *The World Food Shortage*, published in April 1946, the position of the United Kingdom at that time was summarized in the following words:

"The end of the war has brought about a fundamental change in the position of the United Kingdom in relation to the world food situation. During the war the problem was two-fold; first, to cut down imported supplies to a minimum, primarily in order to save shipping; and second, to maintain a regular flow of these minimum supplies in the face

[1] Cmd. 6785

of all the dislocations of war. Broadly speaking, the supplies were there ready to be drawn upon. The United Kingdom was a bastion occupied by great Allied armies into which the nations for whom these armies were fighting were eager to pour supplies in order to maintain the fight.

"With the end of the war, the United Kingdom ceased to occupy that privileged, though perilous position; its claims upon United Nations supplies were now shared by vast liberated areas, some of them parts of the Empire. The wide extension of claimants coincided with a sharp fall in world supplies, due partly to the ravages and claims of war, and partly to an exceptional succession of droughts. Moreover, currency problems which had ceased to be of over-riding importance during the period of Lend-Lease and Mutual Aid again became urgent, and our food imports had once more to be measured carefully in relation to balance of payment and dollar holdings."

In Britain, the food shortage became extremely critical in July 1946, when bread was rationed for the first time in our history. This was followed by a period of extremely bad weather in the winter and spring which reduced the livestock population and resulted in the rationing of potatoes in November 1947.

So acute was the world grain shortage that the United Kingdom had to reduce its imports of wheat by 250,000 tons in the first half of 1946. Before the introduction of bread rationing, the extraction rate had been raised in February 1946, to 82½ per cent, and again in March to 85 per cent. In May, the rate was raised to 90 per cent, but this very high rate was only temporary, as by September 1946 there had been some slight improvement in wheat supplies which enabled the extraction rate to be reduced to 85 per cent towards the end of that month. This reduction in the extraction rate was preferred to any easement of bread rationing, because it enabled the production of animal feedingstuffs obtained from the millers' offals to be increased and thus helped to maintain supplies of milk during the winter. The 85 per cent extraction rate was continued in force until 27 August, 1950, when it was reduced to 80 per cent.

Bread rationing, though the scheme was neither very tight nor very effective and tended to become nominal because it was not strictly enforced as time went on, resulted in a cut of something like 19 lb. a head per annum as compared with 1945.

Consumption in lb. per head per annum

	1945	1946	1947	1948	1949	1950
Flour	240·7	221·8	223·5	232·0	220·7	204·0
Potatoes	260·2	282·0	284·1	237·2	255·5	243·6

Probably some part of the saving in bread was effected by reduced waste and less feeding of bread to animals. There was also for a time a prohibition, often honoured in the breach, against serving bread in restaurants with a main meal which was particularly irksome and of little value in saving bread.

Potato consumption as will be seen from the table above rose greatly in 1946 and 1947, reaching a record figure of 284 lb. a head in 1947. In comparison the highest figure for potato consumption during the war was 275 lb. a head in 1944. This very high rate of potato consumption in 1946 and 1947 was a sure sign that other foods were scarce, and that calorie deficiencies had to be made good by consuming a bulkier diet. It is possible that the efficiency of some workers may have suffered as they may not have been able to consume sufficient of this bulkier and unaccustomed diet to provide for their energy needs. The substitution of 24 lb. of potatoes a head for some 17 lb. of bread a head in 1947 meant the loss on the average of something like 50 calories a day, because bread has approximately six times the energy value of potatoes, weight for weight. The disappointing potato crop of 1947–48 which led to potato rationing in November, brought about a reduction in potato consumption from 284 lb. in 1947 to 237 lb. in 1948. This in turn was in part responsible for a rise to 232 lb. a head in flour consumption in 1948, a figure almost identical with that of 1944.

The improved position in regard to bread grains in 1948 was brought about by an improvement in world harvests, and as will be seen from the table below there was an increase in world production of some 19 million metric tons in 1948 as compared with 1947.

World Production of Bread Grains
Million metric tons

1934–38	1945	1946	1947	1948
148	127	145	143	162

Meat Supplies since the War. The British public, like the infant Hercules who preferred meat to any other food, has always placed a high value on meat. Meat supplies, including bacon and ham, declined steadily from 1946, except for a slight improvement in 1949, but this was followed by a severe set-back in supplies at the end of 1950 and the beginning of 1951 owing to the cessation of supplies from the Argentine. The reduction in the meat ration was severely felt by all classes of the community, and it was probably regarded by the vast majority of the population as the main contributing cause to the impoverishment of the national diet as compared with pre-war standards. From the following table, it will be seen that the greatest decline between 1945 and 1948 was in pork, bacon and ham. Bacon, which was eulogized by Cobbett in the early nineteenth century as "a great softener of the temper and promoter of domestic harmony", has long been the stand-by of the British breakfast table. As no acceptable substitute is available, the smallness of the ration since the end of the war has involved no small sacrifice.

Compared with pre-war, it will be observed that there has been a falling-off in supplies of all types of meat except the canned variety, but even that declined sharply in 1948. There has also been a reduction in the quality of the meat supplied to the British market and complaints have been numerous regarding the high proportion of cow beef and ewe mutton in the ration. The trade in chilled meat has not been revived

Meat Supplies lb. per head per annum

	Pre-war (1934-38)	1945	1946	1947	1948	1949	1950
Beef—bone in	53·0	29·3	33·1	31·9	33·6	34·7	43·0
Beef—bone out	1·7	3·5	10·2	10·1	5·4	3·0	3·2
Mutton and lamb	25·2	25·6	24·3	24·2	22·8	21·9	25·0
Pork	11·5	11·2	3·3	1·0	1·1	2·3	4·3
Offals	7·4	5·6	5·6	5·4	5·6	6·6	6·7
Canned corned meat	2·1	3·5	6·4	6·7	3·9	2·2	2·9
Other canned meat	0·8	4·9	7·3	4·9	2·2	2·8	4·8
Bacon and ham	27·3	16·8	15·1	10·1	10·8	13·5	22·0
Total as edible weight	109·6	86·6	89·9	82·0	73·8	74·6	95·6
As percentage of pre-war	—	79	82	75	67	68	87

Source. Cmd. 7842 and Ministry of Food.

because bulk purchase and rationing require storage, and the delay prevents the meat from being distributed within the maximum period for which it will keep.

In July 1950, Argentine meat shipments to the United Kingdom were suspended because of a dispute over prices, though at first the effects were not so severely felt in this country as might have been expected, because meat shipments had been much heavier than usual in the first half of 1950, owing to a severe summer drought in Argentina which led ranchers to send their cattle in large numbers to the meat-packing stations.

Supplies of meat to the British consumer during 1951 fluctuated violently. In September 1951, the weekly meat ration was 2s. 2d. when home supplies were plentiful and the public failed to take up the whole of its ration, whereas six months earlier, it had been a meagre eightpennyworth. The abundant autumnal supplies did not last long and the ration soon dwindled again. Further, by 1951 the whole system of meat distribution had become over-complicated and was attacked in scathing phrases by *The Economist.*

"It would be hard to imagine a combination of more absurdities than the system which gives the butchers a vested interest in handling less meat, pays them for not selling it, freezes the trade at its pre-war size, although the quantity of meat to be handled is much less and leaves meat piling up at some butchers' while others in wealthier districts could sell twice as much. Never was scarcity organized with such intricate care."[1]

The system, moreover, gave some apparent though specious basis to complaints from overseas that the Ministry of Food was making a profit from imported meat to help to pay the subsidies on home-produced meat.

Fish, Poultry and Game. During the war years, supplies of fish fell off considerably, but they have since been greater than in pre-war days as will be seen from Tables 8 and 11 of the Statistical Appendix. The greater supplies of fish have done something to provide an alternative to meat, and have made it possible for a certain amount of home entertaining to be undertaken, which otherwise the small meat ration might have prevented. Poultry practically reached the pre-war level in 1948, but supplies of game and rabbits were less. Supplies of poultry steadily rose from 2·9 lb. a head per annum in 1945 to 4·3 in 1948 as compared with 4·5 lb. pre-war. Game and rabbit supplies also rose steadily in the same period, but were only 2·5 lb. a head per annum in 1948 as compared with 3·7 lb. in pre-war days.

Oils and Fats. In the oils and fats group, including butter and margarine, there has been a substantial improvement after a set-back in 1946 and 1947 when supplies were only three-quarters of the pre-war amount and were 9 per cent below the lowest level reached during the war years. By 1949 consumption had reached nearly 97 per cent of pre-war, but

[1] *The Economist.* September 22, 1951, p. 670.

within the group there has been a shift from butter to margarine, with the result that the palatibility of the diet has been reduced below that which the figures would at first sight suggest. While the consumption of butter has been halved, that of margarine has been doubled.

Dairy Products. In this group of foodstuffs which includes liquid milk, cheese, evaporated milk, condensed milk and dried milk, the outstanding feature has been the steady and uninterrupted improvement in supplies of liquid milk which have progressively increased each year since 1939, and have broken all previous records in 1950, when for the greater part of the year supplies to the general consumer were unrestricted. This has been achieved, however, in part at the expense of milk products. Cream has not been available since 1940, except for a short period in 1951. Cheese consumption, which reached a peak of 59 per cent above pre-war consumption in 1942, declined almost continuously after that year, and in 1948 fell below the pre-war level due to the reduction of dollar imports. Most of the cheese consumed is still of the uninteresting and unattractive quality which was introduced during the war, but the resumption of imports of fancy cheeses some years ago has made it possible to purchase much better qualities though at a much higher price than the rationed variety. In 1950, a big step forward was achieved when seven varieties of home-produced high-quality cheeses were on sale on the ration for those fortunate enough to obtain them. These are Cheddar, Cheshire, Lancashire, Leicester, Dunlop, Stilton and White Wensleydale, but of these seven varieties Cheshire and Cheddar accounted for some 90 per cent of the increased production and only very small quantities of the others were available.

Other Foods. There has been a steady increase in the consumption of shell eggs, but that of dried eggs has fallen off since 1945 owing to restrictions on dollar imports. Consumption of sugar and syrup has risen steadily from 1945 when consumption was 74 lb. a head to 1949 when consumption reached a figure of 91·1 lb. a head, though this is still considerably below the 110 lb. of pre-war. Vegetable consumption during the years 1946–48 was substantially above pre-war, but it fell in 1949 to approximately the same figure as it was in pre-war days. Fruit on the other hand has not yet reached the pre-war level, being 131 lb. in 1949 as compared with 141 lb. pre-war. This is, however, a marked increase compared with the 91 lb. of 1945 and the 60 lb. of 1941. Pulses and nuts have also failed to attain the pre-war level and have been running at something like two-thirds of pre-war supplies.

Since 1945, there has gradually been some improvement in the supply of the "bits and pieces" which help to make meals more attractive. For example, rice, sago and tapioca have re-appeared and supplies of salad creams, olive oil and table jellies have become available again, while somewhat better supplies of butter, more liquid milk for the general consumer, more shell eggs and more sugar, even though these commodities are not yet available in the quantities that are desired, have done a good deal to make meals more palatable and varied, as compared with the worst of the war years.

Consumption levels are now practically the same as in pre-war years, measured in calories, and there has been an improvement in the consumption of proteins though this has been effected by an increase in vegetable protein consumption. From the health standpoint, it is generally accepted that it is immaterial whether the essential protein units are derived from the vegetable or animal foods though the B.M.A. Committee on nutrition draws attention to the point that the nutritional value of animal foods may be determined in no small measure by the presence of nutrients other than protein. The consumption of fat is, however, still somewhat below that of pre-war days. (See Table 11 in the Statistical Appendix.)

The nutrients in the diet such as calcium, iron, ascorbic acid, Vitamin B1, riboflavin and nicotinic acid, improved considerably from the low point reached in 1941, and in the post-war years have been consistently well above the amounts consumed in pre-war years. The only exception appears to be Vitamin A which until 1948 was below the pre-war figure. (See Table 13 in the Statistical Appendix.)

Though in 1949, the calorie level was about the same as

that in pre-war years, and the nutrient equivalents were substantially above pre-war, the general pattern of the diet was more like that of war-time than that of the pre-war years. Improvements in the nutrients and the maintenance of the calorie values of the average diet have only been attained by a change in its pattern. The consumption of the more bulky and less palatable foods has increased and for some of them the consumption per head is even greater than it was before the First World War. In this respect, the position has deteriorated, and the standard has been brought back below the standard of the pattern of food consumption of 1909–13. According to A. W. Flux the consumption of wheat flour in the period 1909–13 was 211 lb. a head per annum, whereas in 1950 it was 204 lb. a head per annum, and for potatoes the figures were 208 lb. a head per annum in 1909–13, and 244 lb. in 1950. It is probably true that the diet has improved in other respects, but it is clear that the trends in the pattern of the diet which had been evolving since 1913 have been arrested and indeed to this extent reversed. It would seem that we are consuming more bread, more potatoes, less butter and less meat on the average than before the First World War.

There is, however, a smaller spread around the average and the food consumption of different classes is obviously more uniform. A considerable improvement has taken place in the diet of the "lower income groups" while that of the "higher income groups" has fallen considerably. Rationing, food subsidies, "full employment" and the redistribution of incomes have led to a much greater degree of uniformity; fewer fall much below the average for their age or sex, but few rise much above the average. The raising of the standard of the poorest fed along with the improvement in the diet of children and expectant and nursing mothers have been among the great social achievements of the war and post-war periods. In this, increased knowledge of nutrition has played a considerable part.

The Problem of Currency. During the war, the main problem connected with the procurement of supplies of food from overseas was that of obtaining adequate shipping. When our financial reserves were giving out, Lend-Lease came to our aid and there was, therefore, no acute currency problem to be faced. Immediately after the war, the world food crisis prevented adequate supplies being obtained, though even then there were ominous signs that we would be faced with the problem of finding the necessary dollars to buy food where it was most readily available. The cessation of Lend-Lease created a serious problem of supply and when in 1947 the American loan began to run out and a balance of payments crisis occurred, drastic cuts had to be made in supplies from dollar sources and hard currency areas. This change was the more serious because during the war years, there had been a marked swing over to United States sources of supply. The

SOURCES OF U.K. IMPORTS OF FOOD

(*Analysis of Value*)

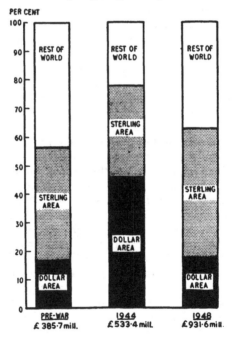

PER CENT

| PRE-WAR | 1944 | 1948 |
| £ 385·7 mill. | £ 533·4 mill. | £ 931·6 mill. |

general pattern of the changes which have taken place in the sources of supply is shown in Table 2 in the Statistical Appendix and in the diagram opposite.

Britain has been forced to turn more and more to the sterling area for food supplies and but for Marshall Aid and the Canadian Credit would have had to curtail even further her purchases from North America. Before the war, Britain obtained about 16 per cent of her total food imports from dollar sources. In 1946, the proportion had risen to 36 per cent. Since then dependence on dollar imports has been greatly reduced, and by the end of 1949 only 12 per cent of Britain's food came from dollar sources, and of that figure wheat accounted for 9 per cent. In 1949 Canada supplied nearly two-thirds of our total requirements of wheat. By 1950, the process of reducing dollar imports had gone so far that apart from comparatively small quantities of bacon and cheese from Canada and of sugar from the Caribbean, the only food for which Britain was paying a substantial amount of dollars was wheat.

Shortage of dollars has, however, complicated the problem of food purchase as Britain has sometimes been prevented as a result from buying in the cheapest market. The sterling area and the dollar area for certain foodstuffs became to all intents and purposes separate watertight compartments which were only partially bridged by Marshall Aid. The fall in the price of fats in the dollar area, exaggerated by shortage of dollars elsewhere, was the most remarkable example of divergence in price as fats were much dearer in the sterling area.

As an offset to the rigidities in world trade which have resulted from dollar shortages, there has been a certain liberalization of trade in Western Europe as part of the programme of O.E.E.C. and the work of the European Payments Union, though this increase in international trade provides only a partial counter-balance to the reduction in dollar imports. As a result, however, there has been during the last year or two an increasing quantity and variety of imported delicacies to be obtained in this country, including French, Italian and other cheeses, Danish biscuits, Dutch and Belgian chocolate,

Frankfürter sausages and French, Dutch and other canned goods, including ham. Writing in the *Manchester Guardian* of 5 March 1951, their London Correspondent was able to describe Soho as a "Land of Plenty" as a result of this increase in imported specialities from Europe. The Soho restaurants, he said, had a plenitude of everything except fresh butcher's meat, though to us "accustomed for generations to cheap imported food, the prices charged in first-class restaurants everywhere are staggering. Even the cost of the delicacies in the Soho shops is greater than most of us are willing to pay, except for an occasional treat. Yet what a picture they make. In every window there are monuments of cheese, and the Italian grocer with an eye for chiaroscuro surrounds the Stilton, that delicately blue-veined English aristocrat, with the sombre-rinded Parmesan. The bottles of olive oil glow with a gold as pure as that of the French wines next door, and the sausages, wrapped in silver or multi-coloured foil, are like a Christmas decoration. . . . In the background are tins with coloured labels that show they come from all the lands of Europe." The import cuts announced early in 1952 will unfortunately reduce the variety of these unrationed foods.

In the post-war period the terms of trade have turned against this country, and now a given quantity of food imports requires a larger quantity of our exports. To some extent, this has been met by a shift to cheaper items of food. In 1949, it had been expected that the cost of Britain's imported food would fall and indeed for a time in 1950 it seemed that this forecast would be borne out when cereal prices tended to sag, and there was a remarkable fall in the price of fats in the United States. These prospects of cheaper food faded as the year progressed and practically all exporting countries, including those in the Commonwealth, began to make vigorous attempts to obtain higher prices. It was of course in any case inevitable that the devaluation of the pound, effected in 1949, should have had an adverse effect on the prices of imports from dollar sources.

In 1950 and 1951 the Korean War, and re-armament with its stockpiling programmes, led to a marked rise in world prices, and though foodstuffs were not affected to the same extent as other raw materials, the higher prices demanded for food imports added greatly to Britain's food problems. The extremely high price of wool had adverse reactions on meat supply, as farmers were encouraged to keep their sheep for another year's shearing rather than to sell them for slaughtering.

It is at the present time only too clear that if Britain's food imports are to be increased, overseas suppliers will have to be offered better inducements. Complaints are frequently made that Britain has raised the price of her own exports of coal and manufactured goods much more than the prices she is prepared to pay for meat and dairy products.

Home Production of Food. British farming is technically highly efficient, though there are considerable variations in the efficiency with which Britain's 400,000 farms of every size and shape are farmed. Only in a very few countries, notably the Netherlands, Denmark and Belgium, are higher yields per acre or more milk per cow obtained than in Britain, and even then the yield is only slightly higher. There is, of course, something to be learnt from these countries, but their high yields are largely obtained by intensive application of manpower. The output per worker in British agriculture is higher than that of any other European country, though less than in the Middle Western States of the U.S.A., in Western Canada and in Australia. In those countries, however, cultivation is less intensive and yields per acre are lower. Britain has now more tractor power per acre than any other country in the world. Emphasizing this point, Sir John Russell stated in his Presidential Address to the British Association for the Advancement of Science at its Newcastle Meeting in 1949 that "Perhaps the most significant changes in modern farming have been the increasing mechanization and the alacrity with which the younger farmers have accepted it. Tractors are displacing working horses—perhaps too rapidly. Before the war about 60,000 tractors and 650,000 horses were used in Great Britain's agriculture. In 1948 there were over 260,000 tractors, mostly ranging from 12 to 40 h.p., a gain of more than 200,000. Assuming with the Oxford Agricultural Economics Research

Institute that the effective working power of one tractor is, on the average, the equivalent of four horses, our farms had in 1948 1¼ million 'horse equivalents' compared with the pre-war 889,000, a gain of 68 per cent."

British agriculture over the past 50 years has shown a considerable increase in average crop yields as will be seen from the following table. The increase in the last ten years is the

Average yields in Great Britain in bushels per acre

	1885–94	1929–38	1940–49
Wheat	29·3	32·5	35·8
Barley	43·0	33·9	40·1
Oats	38·2	44·8	47·7

Source. *Prospect for the Land.* Text by L. F. Easterbrook. Prepared by the Economic Information Unit and the Central Office of Information.

more remarkable, especially in wheat, as during the war years and since, grain has been grown on less suitable lands with the object of increasing home supplies. Moreover, British agriculture even in 1885 was highly efficient, and cheap labour was then available for hand-weeding. In comparison with British yields to-day, American yields are about 13½ bushels of wheat per acre, 23 of barley and 30 of oats.

Home agriculture has a very important part to play in the feeding of the nation, but in the nature of things, given our climatic and topographical conditions, the main contribution of Britain's agriculture must lie in the provision of livestock products, milk, maincrop potatoes, vegetables and the "protective foodstuffs" generally. Britain's best and most valuable crop is grass, and grass means livestock, though grass-feeding needs to be supplemented by barley, oats and mixed corn. Ley farming is recommended by many agricultural experts on the grounds that it would enable the best balance to be kept between arable and livestock farming. To meet the winter needs of cattle and sheep, silage and grass-drying present great possibilities.

During the war, British agriculture had been set the task of reducing the country's dependence on shipments of food from overseas, and for this purpose emphasis had been placed on the production of cereals, potatoes, sugar beet and fodder crops. The emphasis since the end of the war, and more especially since 1947, shifted to the saving of dollars and hard currencies, instead of shipping space. During the war, pigs, poultry and sheep had been greatly reduced in number, but now the need for pigmeat, eggs and mutton has led to a policy for the revival and expansion of the livestock industry.

Immediately after the war, there was some falling off in agricultural output, and the proportion of home-produced food reached a low level of 35 per cent in 1947–48 as the calorie contribution from home agriculture was reduced by a poor potato crop. Since then, there has been a recovery and the proportion has been about 40 per cent as compared with the 31 per cent of pre-war days. The severe winter of 1947 brought a slight set-back in the production of milk, which had been steadily increasing since 1941. By 1948 the difficulties had been overcome and total production was some 1,839 million gallons compared with 1,716 million gallons in 1939. Average yield per cow in the meantime had risen from 551 gallons to 562 gallons, the highest on record.

The Agricultural Expansion Programme. In August 1947 an ambitious four-years' programme of agricultural expansion was announced which had as its main objective the reduction of our dependence on imported foods from hard currency areas and was designed to increase the net agricultural output by £100 million, that is, 20 per cent, by 1951–52. It was expected that half of the increase in output would be secured as a result of increased efficiency which it was envisaged would amount to about 2 per cent per annum. The remaining £50 million, it was intended, should come from additions to the resources of the industry. It was not envisaged that expansion would be uniform, product by product; rather emphasis was deliberately placed on dollar-saving products, particularly pigmeat, eggs, beef, mutton, cereals and linseed. The programme was essentially one of reviving and expanding the production of meat and eggs, restoring part of the war-time expansion of wheat and barley and adding 400,000 acres of linseed, a product little grown in this country in pre-war years. New subsidies were introduced with the object of securing an increase in the tillage area, expanding the acreage of temporary leys, improving their quality and securing conservation of the grass for winter feeding of cattle and sheep and encouraging the rearing of young cattle for both the beef and dairy industries. There was a subsidy of £4 an acre for grasslands ploughed up, or re-sown, and another of £4 a head for steer calves, and £3 a head for heifer calves of approved types if reared to 12 months old. Financial assistance was also promised for the purpose of encouraging grass conservation, and improving cattle breeds.

A grassland improvement campaign was initiated at the same time which aimed at the eventual contribution of the equivalent of an additional 1½ million tons of feedingstuffs a year.

During the four years of the Expansion Programme, livestock production as a whole was considerably increased. By 1950, there were nearly as many sheep as there were before the disastrous winter of 1946–47, and nearly half-a-million additional acres were under wheat in England and Wales. Poultry flocks, which had continued to expand since the end of the war, had risen to over 53 million head in 1950. During the last year of the Programme, there was a spectacular rise in the pig population and a moderate increase in the number of sheep and beef cattle, offset by a small decline in milk production. This change in emphasis had been deliberately engineered at the February Price Review of 1951 to fit in with changing needs. Coarse grains for use as animal feedingstuffs had not, however, increased to the extent which had been hoped. The area under main crops declined after 1948 and many farmers for various reasons seem reluctant to intensify production of crops beyond the point reached in 1948. Imported supplies come from hard currency areas or the U.S.S.R. and our ability to secure them has not been great. This has limited further livestock expansion.

The expansion of home agricultural production has to be related to cost, and there are critics of the present system who point out that while it is true that the subsidies may only suffice to make it worth the while of some farmers to expand production, others are more than sufficiently compensated. If the present system of stimulating increased output by financial incentives were to be expanded, it would undoubtedly involve still higher costs than at present. Farms which show the highest output levels could only expand their production at higher costs, and it has been estimated by C. H. Blagburn[1], from a sample investigation of such farms, that replacement of foreign supplies requires the use of about 11 acres of land, and about £120 worth of other indigenous resources for every £100 net import equivalent.

There would seem to be room for a considerable expansion of home agricultural production if means can be devised for stimulating greater output among the less efficient farmers as for example, by transferring some of the funds at present utilized in subsidizing prices, to improving the efficiency and output of low-output farms, or by exerting pressure on the less efficient farmers under the efficiency provisions of the Agriculture Act. Something also might be done by means of improved agricultural education and advisory work. There is evidence that a majority of farmers would find it profitable to expand their output on the basis of present (1952) prices. In a sample study, C. H. Blagburn found that farm expenditure tended to increase much less rapidly than the value of output.[2]

The old adage, "High farming, high profits: Low farming, low profits" is still substantially true. British farming to-day like British industry shows the traditional mixture of some highly efficient units and a majority of units well below the standard of management and organization for their size and type which is reached by the best.

The sequence of events which led to the introduction of the 1947 Expansion Programme was repeated in 1952 and the Government had once again to try urgently to expand home production. A special subsidy of £5 an acre towards the cost

[1] "Import Replacement by British Agriculture," *Economic Journal*, March 1950. No. 237.
[2] *Some Economic Aspects of Increasing Farm Output.*

of ploughing up old grassland and sowing it to an approved crop was introduced in February 1952 with the aim of increasing meat production by improving the supply of home-grown feedingstuffs.

National Expenditure on Food. The annual White Papers on National Income and Expenditure provide a broad picture of the nation's expenditure on food. In 1938 food, other than alcoholic beverages, accounted for 30 per cent of total personal expenditure, but in 1948 this had fallen to 27 per cent. In 1949, the percentage increased to 28 per cent, showing that food was taking a somewhat larger share of personal expenditure, like clothing. The necessary re-adjustments were, it would seem, effected largely on the items in the alcoholic beverages and tobacco group and in the entertainment, books, etc. group. Though the percentage allocation of expenditure on food was smaller than in pre-war years, total expenditure on food rose from £1,305 million in 1938 to £2,048 million in 1947, £2,221 million in 1948 and £2,381 million in 1949. With larger incomes, in other words, the proportion of the income spent on food declined, which at first sight would seem to be a confirmation in a generalized sense of Engel's Law that "the poorer the family the more spent on food", meaning that the lower the income the greater the proportion that has to be spent on food. It should be remembered, however, that food has become heavily subsidized since 1938, and has been rationed and controlled in various ways. Averaged over the whole population, weekly household expenditure on food (excluding expenditure outside the home) worked out at 9s. 8d. a head in 1938, at about 15s. in 1948 and at just over 16s. in 1949. The White Paper on National Income and Expenditure provides an estimate of 1948 consumption valued at 1938 prices, and this shows that there was a rise of 63 per cent in food prices between 1938 and 1948, though full allowance cannot be made for changes in variety, quality and associated services. Other prices, however, rose much more, the average for all consumers' goods and services being 80 per cent, though here again full allowance cannot be made for changes in quality.

As has been explained above, the fall in the proportion of incomes spent on food is due largely to the heavy subsidization of food. For the year 1948 the net amount of subsidies on food, after deducting Customs and Excise Duties, was £358 million, equivalent to about 2s. 9d. a head a week.

If the cost of subsidies specific to food is added to the total personal expenditure on food, and customs and excise duties on food are deducted, we arrive at the cost to the nation of its food. This basic or factor cost is calculated in the White Papers. The term factor cost is used because it is the cost of employing all the factors of production to obtain the nation's food. In total personal expenditure what is measured is the cost of the food to the individual, not the true cost to the nation of its food. The national cost of food in 1949 was £2,748 million as compared with total personal expenditure on food of £2,381. In 1938 the respective totals were £1,267 and £1,305. For the detailed figures relating to national expenditure, the reader is referred to Tables 21 and 22 in the Statistical Appendix.

Food subsidies which were developed during the war to stabilize the cost of living and to secure cheap food so that none should want the minimum necessities of a good diet, grew at a dangerous rate after the war. In 1939–40 the annual cost of food subsidies was something like £13 million, and by 1943–44 the cost had increased to some £187 million. In the post-war period, the cost of subsidies increased year by year until it reached the enormous total of £484·4 million in 1948–49, when the Chancellor of the Exchequer was forced to impose a limit of £465 million. Thereafter the food subsidies were held within this limit, and amounted to about £440 million in 1949–50 and some £410 million in 1950–51. It is estimated that food subsidies represented about 2s. 8d. a head a week in 1946–47, and about 3s. 8d. in mid-1948. (See Tables 17 to 20 in the Statistical Appendix for details of the amounts of the subsidies.)

The subsidization of food placed the country in a serious dilemma. If subsidies were reduced to a minimum or entirely eliminated, a demand for increased wages might have set in train an inflationary spiral, despite the fact that all tax-payers in varying degrees would have had greater disposable incomes in their hands. On the other hand, the dead weight of the subsidies expenditure involved continued taxation at a high rate, with its restrictions on choice of expenditure on the part of income-earners, and the disincentive effects of the high taxation itself. Had world prices of food and the cost of home production of food fallen the subsidies could have been gradually withdrawn, and at the same time the cost of living as shown by the official price index numbers would have remained unaffected. This did not happen, and on the contrary, the cost of buying the nation's food increased seriously. Subsidization also had another serious implication in that any increase of the ration of subsidized foodstuffs automatically increased the amount of the expenditure on subsidies. Obviously the dilemma of the subsidies could only be solved by bold action, but it was not until the March Budget of 1952 that the nettle was firmly grasped. Food subsidies were then cut down to a total of £250 million for the year 1952–53, that is by an amount of £160 million from the previous total of £410 million. It was estimated that the reduction in subsidies would mean a rise of about 1s. 6d. a head a week in the cost of living. Had the position been left at this, demands for higher wages and salaries would have been inevitable, but in compensation for the reduction of subsidies, income tax reliefs were increased as were family allowances and pensions. Thus the persons most likely to be seriously affected by the reduction of subsidies were safeguarded while at the same time the prices of foods such as bread, flour, meat, fats, cheese, butter, sugar, bacon and eggs were brought more into line with their real costs.

Household Food Survey. Much valuable information has been collected by the Ministry of Food through its household food survey which had its origin in the war-time need to keep a watch on food consumption in the home, so that any signs of under-nutrition might be brought to light. This survey provides information of the daily consumption of and expenditure on each food for a large sample of urban working-class families.

In Tables 15 and 16 in the Statistical Appendix, some information from this Survey is summarized. It will be seen that there has been a fairly steady increase in milk consumption except for a small recession in 1947, consumption having increased from 3·5 pints a head per week in 1942 to 4·4 pints in 1949. Sugar consumption also showed a steady rise from 8·4 oz. a head a week in 1942 to 10·9 oz. in 1949, though cheese declined steadily from 3·6 oz. a head a week in 1942 to 2 oz. in 1948, and then rose to 2·2 oz. in 1949. Potato consumption reached its maximum in 1946 at 73·8 oz. a head a week when bread rationing reduced somewhat the consumption of bread and flour. Potato consumption fell subsequently, due no doubt to shortage of supplies, but rose again to 68·9 oz. in 1949. Meat consumption was about 23 oz. a head a week in 1948 and 1949, as compared with 28·3 oz. in 1944. The consumption of fruit showed a great increase in 1947 when it was 21·7 oz. a head a week as compared with 15·7 oz in 1946, and only 12 oz. in 1942. Thereafter consumption fell somewhat to 22.4 oz. in 1949. Egg consumption fell off after 1945 owing to the virtual disappearance of dried egg, which is a dollar import, but consumption recovered in 1949 when it was practically the same as in 1945 due to the increase in home production of eggs.

Food expenditure according to the survey rose steadily from 111 pence per head per week in 1942, to 164 pence in 1949, that is by very nearly 50 per cent. No comparable figure can be given for pre-war expenditure, but this might be taken as round about 105 pence judging from information contained in the Ministry of Labour Budgets relating to average expenditure per head on food consumed in the home.

Cost of Living Index. The Ministry of Labour published a cost of living index (July 1914 = 100) until June 1947, when the food component was 17 per cent above the September 1939 level. The weighting of this index was based on the sample of working-class family budgets collected in 1904, and only 14 foods were included. The disparity between the cost of living index and the index of price changes shown in the White Paper on National Expenditure arose mainly from the limited

cover of the cost of living index, and from the fact that it was
weighted in favour of those foods which formed the basis of
the national diet and had therefore been subsidized.

When the cost of living index was discontinued, a new interim index of retail prices (17 June 1947 = 100) was introduced, in which the food component was given a weight of
34·8 per cent. The food component as is also the case with
other commodities cannot be linked with the old cost of living
index number, because of difference in coverage and weighing.
The food items included in the old index represented only
about 20 per cent of the weighting assigned to the much longer
list of commodities in the new index. The interim index is
intended to serve only as a temporary index until such time
as a permanent index can be introduced, when the expenditure of working-class households can be recorded in a market
considerably more free than when the temporary index was
constructed. The weights given to the interim index have been
calculated according to the pre-war pattern of consumption
disclosed by the family budget inquiry undertaken by the
Ministry of Labour in 1937–38.[1]

The Cost of Living Advisory Committee set up by the
Ministry of Labour and National Service in March 1947, in
their first Interim Report (Cmd. 7077) left open the question
of the form which the permanent index should take. Opinion
among statisticians is now coming to the view that the best
index would be one in which the weighting would be revised
at frequent intervals, since a monthly retail price index is
essentially a method of comparing changes over a few years
rather than over long periods. It is felt, therefore, that it
should be kept closely related to the current habits of consumers and that the "basket of goods" which it uses as the basis
for weighting should be revised say every five years preferably
in the same year as the census is taken. There is also a strong
case for making the index a "national index" and not merely
a "working-class" index. There has long been a need for in-

[1] For a full account of the method of construction and calculation of the
interim index of retail prices see a publication entitled *Interim Index of
Retail Prices* issued by H.M.S.O. in 1950.

dices which would shed some light on the effects of retail price changes on different groups within the community, such as families of different sizes, old people and other income or social groups. This is reinforced by the experience of the Ministry of Food in connection with its Household Food Survey. The survey of urban working-class households did not give a sufficiently accurate picture of what was happening, and it was found desirable to institute special inquiries from time to time among such groups as old age pensioners, rural households, coal miners, middle-class households and other groups. It is also very desirable that the information collected from the co-operating families in any quinquennial investigation should include statistics of income as well as expenditure, despite the obvious difficulties which may be encountered in obtaining such information. In a turnover article in *The Times* newspaper of 7 February 1951, it was stated: "In times of stringency, it is in many ways more important to have such budgets comprising the sources of income as well as the channels of outlay, than it is to have any indices which might be based upon them. They would illuminate a great many obscure corners in contemporary life. They would give all concerned with the many hard decisions that lie ahead in social, economic and fiscal policy a clearer understanding of many issues now clouded in opinion. What contribution is made to the standard of living of households of different kinds by particular subsidies which may have to be cut or withdrawn? What is the true value of social insurance, family allowances, rent subsidies and other social benefits which may have to be modified?" The article concluded that an up-to-date set of household budgets drawn from all sections of the community would be of great value, even without a revised index of retail prices, and that it was not an academic luxury, but a real practical administrative requirement "for the good government of a community which wants to equip itself for defence without sacrificing the essentials of the welfare state".

In August 1951, the Cost of Living Advisory Committee issued a second Interim Report[1] recommending a new budget-

[1] Cmd. 8328.

ary inquiry, covering as far as possible all wage-earners and moderate salary-earners. They believed that definite long-term changes in spending habits were emerging as a result of changes in the distribution of income, the introduction of social security schemes and changes in the way of living, and that, therefore, weights calculated from a new full-scale budget inquiry would provide a better basis for an index number than those at present in use. They rejected proposals for a separate middle-class index and for regional indices on the ground that there would be confusion if two or more official monthly indices were published. They suggested, however, that the inquiry should be comprehensive, covering a sample of the whole population and extending beyond the needs of the index number so as to provide information about the pattern of expenditure of all classes and sections of the community. The recommendations of the Committee were accepted by the Ministry of Labour and a large-scale inquiry is to be undertaken into the spending habits of the community which, it is expected, will take two years to complete.

Implementing a further report[1] of the Cost of Living Advisory Committee, certain changes were made as from February 1952, in the weighting of the interim index so as to bring it more into line with current patterns of consumption. Ultimately, this interim index will be replaced by a permanent index based on the results of the new budget inquiry by selecting those households where the head earns from about £150 to £1,000 a year. The obvious criticism is that within such a wide range of incomes, the patterns of expenditure must vary greatly and an index may not retain the confidence of the public unless it reflects the experience of those whose variations in the cost of living it purports to represent.

Cmd. 8481, March 1952.

CHAPTER ELEVEN

The World's Food Supplies

As Britain more than any other country depends on imports of food to meet her requirements, some examination of the world position is desirable in any review of Britain's food problems.

Looking back over the past hundred years, there has been a striking development in the living standards of the advanced countries which among them contain something like one-quarter of the world's population. Until comparatively recently, the peoples of most countries lived on a precarious margin of subsistence as is shown by the periodical occurrence of dearths and famines. To-day, in the advanced countries, diets are diversified, and agriculture has been reorganized to meet rising demands for livestock products, vegetables, fruit, fats, fish and sugar.

But though in these advanced countries the ordinary man can to-day buy more and better food than his parents or grandparents, the other three-quarters of the world's population has been little affected by these changes, and the people in the majority of the under-developed countries live no better than did their ill-nourished ancestors.

Coincident with these variations in diet, standards of agricultural efficiency vary immensely, and the output of food per worker is sometimes ten times greater in advanced countries than in more backward lands. The comparison was put vividly in a Survey by F.A.O. some three or four years ago by showing that in the advanced countries one farm family feeds itself and four other families at a comparatively high nutritional level, whereas in many of the less developed countries, one farm family manages to produce only enough to feed itself and half of another family at a much inferior standard.

So low is the present level of productivity in many countries that relatively simple improvements such as better hand tools, better seed, crop rotations, some fertilizers and insecticides and simple pumps for irrigation would enable production to be increased by 10 to 20 per cent or even 50 per cent in a comparatively short time.

The world food problem is not a uniform single problem but varies from region to region and any appraisal which is to be of value therefore necessitates a break-down of the problem by regions. For convenience these regions may be taken broadly to coincide with the continental areas though a further sub-division would be necessary for a complete detailed picture. It is proposed to consider in this chapter Europe, North America, South America, Australia and New Zealand, the Middle East, Africa and India and the Far East, though it is possible, if a sense of proportion is to be maintained, to survey each of these areas only in the broadest terms.

Europe. The European Continent considered as a whole is the most intensely farmed large region of the world. This is the result of a combination of factors, including rich soils and favourable climate, population pressure and technical efficiency. There are, however, wide variations in types of farming productivity and standards of living. Output per acre in North-West Europe for example is nearly three times as high as in South-East Europe. Mixed livestock farming is characteristic of Western-European farming, whereas in East and South-East Europe the dominant feature is the extensive cultivation of grain crops.

During the first half of the nineteenth century, Western Europe was virtually self-sufficient in food supplies. Though population was growing rapidly, food production was also increasing and millions of acres of waste land were brought into cultivation. The area under fallow was substantially reduced and crop yields were raised two or three-fold as a result of seed selection, improvements in soil fertility brought about by the introduction of clover and root crops, and later by the use of artificial fertilizers. Improved breeds of livestock were introduced, and the output of milk and meat was almost doubled. By 1870 self-sufficiency began to give way to increasing imports, especially from the New World which were facilitated by improvements in transport. Between 1880 and 1930 Germany's food imports increased threefold, those of Belgium, Denmark, Switzerland and Great Britain more than doubled, and those of France increased by more than 50 per cent despite greater home production.

European Agriculture

	Percentage increase 1880–1930		Percentage self-sufficient
	Out-put of Cereals[1]	Live Stock Numbers[2]	1939[3]
Denmark	60	134	105
Netherlands	39	74	72
Switzerland	n.a.	43	52
Germany	44	19	87
Belgium	29	27	51
France	0	19	86

Before the Second World War, Continental Europe on its pre-war boundaries was just over 90 per cent self-sufficient in food supplies compared with the 30 per cent of the U.K. Within the Continental area there were sizeable movements of foodstuffs as, for example, grain and animals from East and South-East Europe to the West, or sugar from Czechoslovakia. There was also considerable international trading in European meat, dairy products, fruit and vegetables. On balance, Europe was a net importer of food and feeding stuffs, amounting in bread grains to 9½ million tons, of which 5¼ million tons went to the U.K., over 10 million tons of coarse grains (4 million tons to the U.K.), over 2 million tons of sugar (1¾ million tons U.K.), and some 7 million tons of oilseeds (1½ million tons U.K.).

During the years between the two world wars both crop and

---

[1] Total of wheat, rye, barley and oats. [2] In livestock units, Cattle = 1, Pigs = 0·2, Sheep = 0·1. [3] Exports offset against imports. Fodder imports reckoned at calorie value of the livestock products they produce.

livestock production continued to expand, but they fell considerably during the Second World War except in the U.K., where there was a considerable increase in grain, potato and sugar beet production. A gradual recovery has taken place in Continental Europe since the end of the war, and by 1948 grain production had reached 90 per cent of pre-war, potatoes 100 per cent and sugar 101 per cent. European cattle numbers by 1951 were almost 90 per cent of their pre-war level, though pigs had reached only 70 per cent.

The U.K. drew upon Continental Europe in pre-war days for ¼ million tons of wheat, about ¼ million tons each of barley, maize, bacon, butter and citrus fruits and about 100,000 tons of eggs. The war cut off these supplies and the re-opening of the former trade has been slow, though pre-war levels of imports of butter, bacon and eggs from Denmark, the Netherlands, and Poland should soon be achieved. France is planning to become a large-scale exporter of meat, dairy products and wheat. Improvements in Western European agriculture are receiving the close attention of O.E.E.C., and the increased production of animal feedingstuffs is being encouraged so as to save not only imports of livestock products, but also imports of the feedingstuffs themselves. It is believed that output from grasslands could be increased by as much as 40 per cent by better methods of cultivation. The Agricultural Expansion Programme of the U.K. aims at increasing production to 150 per cent of the pre-war level by 1952, and the grassland improvement scheme envisages a saving in fodder imports by providing the equivalent of 1½ million tons of feeding stuffs.

The real problem of European farming is to be found not in the West, but in the non-industrial countries of Eastern Europe. These countries have never adopted the intensive farming methods of Western Europe, and though in pre-war days they were considerable exporters of grain and other foodstuffs, the bulk of their populations lived in extreme poverty and overcrowding. These territories have now entered the Russian orbit, and considerable internal changes have taken place. The industrialization which is proceeding may eventually provide a solution of the problem of over-population of the rural areas, but the low productivity of agriculture is bound to continue until the cultivators acquire a knowledge of modern farming techniques. Poland, where almost all the land is still in private hands, may become an important exporter of food once the war-time devastation is overcome, and production is restored to what it was before the war.

Total European population rose from 370 millions in 1928 to nearly 400 millions in 1938. It is now some 390 millions as a result of heavy war casualties and post-war boundary changes, though in certain countries there has been a high rate of population increase. In the Netherlands population has risen from 8·6 millions before the war to 10 millions now; in Italy from 43 millions to 47½ millions, while in Germany to-day 70 million people are living where formerly there were only 60½ millions. Poland on the other hand has to-day only 24 millions as compared with 34 millions pre-war, and Czechoslovakia 12½ millions in place of 14½ millions.

North America. In contrast to Europe, land in North America is more plentiful and population densities are much lower. Farming is less intensive and efficiency, at any rate as measured by crop yields, is lower than in such European countries as the U.K. and Denmark. Should need arise, more intensive cultivation would permit very substantial increases in production to be effected. Broadly speaking, the U.S. is self-sufficient in food production, while Canada produces a large exportable surplus. During the war, food production was raised to a high level, especially in the U.S., and this was maintained until 1948. The official index of the yield of 53 crops in the U.S. rose from 96·4 in 1930 (1923–32 = 100) to a record level of 137·2 in 1948, but fell in 1949 to 130. Increased production has been obtained by improved methods of crop and animal husbandry, enabling larger output per acre to be obtained. Canadian wheat production rose from a long-term average of 8 million long tons to a peak of 15 millions in 1942, but since then a downward trend has been evident owing to less favourable weather. During the war the U.S. became a net exporter, but is not likely to continue so, and the most recent trade returns show diminished exports particularly in grains.

Canadian food exports consist of grains (especially wheat), fresh and canned fruits, fish, cheese and processed milk. During the war, exports of eggs and bacon also became important. Post-war developments have upset the normal pattern of trade whereby Canada's favourable balance of trade with the U.K. was used to liquidate her indebtedness to the U.S.A. This is now prevented by inconvertibility of sterling and Canadian trade policy has had to be substantially modified.

The problem of surpluses is unquestionably the main future problem for North American agriculture. The U.S. Agricultural Act, 1949, reintroduced acreage allotments and marketing quotas which had been largely abandoned because of war requirements. Support prices are to be provided after 1950 on a sliding scale, and increasing emphasis is likely to be placed on livestock production, involving some reduction in grain and oilseeds. Marshall Aid enabled European countries to absorb U.S. farm surpluses, but when this and similar assistance ceases, the U.S. will have to decide on a policy to meet the situation which will result from the loss of an important outlet for agricultural products. Several courses of action are open to the U.S. Administration. The first would be a withdrawal from world markets, but this would involve restriction of production, and if it took place before production elsewhere in the world had increased it would involve shortage and high prices for importing countries. A return to free international trading with abolition of price support and production restrictions, and the release of U.S. agricultural surpluses upon world markets at competitive prices, is not a very likely policy in view of U.S. experience in the depression of the 1930's. Other possible courses of action are the introduction of some international agency which would absorb and dispense surplus food production, or the donation of surpluses to needy countries while maintaining home prices. Among schemes of donating surpluses now being canvassed is one for giving supplies to those Asiatic countries which undertake to raise their low standards of cultivation and productivity, but none of the schemes so far put forward seem to safeguard the legitimate interest of importing countries in obtaining commercial supplies at prices which do not distort their terms of trade. The question of surpluses has, however, recently taken on a new aspect as a result of the re-armament drive and the promise of assistance to the Atlantic Pact countries under the Mutual Security Plan. Ultimate decisions have therefore been postponed for the time being.

Population trends have been upwards in both Canada and the U.S. during the past 20 years, and there has at the same time been migration from rural to urban areas. U.S. population was 122 millions in 1922, but rose to 149 millions in 1949, while Canada's population rose in the same period from 10 millions to nearly 14 millions.

South America. The countries of South America are traditionally exporters of many primary products, notably meat and coffee, but they are deficit countries for those foods which require intensive production methods or skills beyond that of the average peasant producer. Argentina ranks with Canada as one of the two most important surplus food-producing areas of the world. Costs of agricultural production, however, have been rising steeply during the past 20 years without any proportionate increase in productivity. Mechanization on a large scale could have transformed Argentina's agriculture, but the Government monopoly has diverted the profits of agricultural production to industrial and other developments. It has been estimated that at least 400,000 tractors could have been usefully employed on the present cultivated area.

The Argentine exportable surplus of meat is an important item in U.K. supplies, but the U.K. is becoming increasingly independent of Argentine produce. Meat production seems in danger of declining like that of wheat and maize, the exports of which in 1948 were only half as large as those made in 1934. Areas sown to linseed have also declined, though rye, barley and rice have shown an upward trend. Within the Argentine, consumption of meat has risen greatly as a result of the policy of favouring industry at the expense of agriculture. Future trends, however, are difficult to forecast since Argentine Government policy is changeable, and much has recently been promised by the Government to the agricultural industry.

Beef and mutton are produced for the U.K. in Uruguay to the extent roughly of 10,000 tons per annum. There is generally no export of wheat as the country is mainly pastoral. Since the war there has been a trend towards more intensive farming and pasture is now being ploughed up for sowing to wheat and linseed.

Brazil is the world's greatest producer of coffee, and has tended to dominate world prices in that commodity. The long-continued decline in the Brazilian coffee harvest from nearly 1¼ million tons pre-war to under 1 million tons in 1949 has led to a great rise in world prices of coffee. There is likely on the other hand to be a considerable increase in cocoa bean production during the next few years in Brazil, and this is an important development in view of the threat of the swollen shoot disease in the Gold Coast plantations. Brazil imports wheat and wheaten flour, but in addition to coffee and cocoa, exports maize, rice, bran, sugar, meat and fruit.

Argentina, with 14 persons to the square mile, is under-populated, though her population increased by 4 millions between 1933 and 1947. Uruguay, on the other hand, is fairly densely populated, carrying over 2 million people on 3½ million acres of cultivated land. Wool export dominates her economy, and her economic future is largely linked to the world demand for wool. Brazil, though containing nearly half the total population of South America, is still a "frontier" farming country, and only 4 per cent of her enormous area—equal to the size of Europe without Russia—is under cultivation.

Australia and New Zealand. Australia, like Brazil, is a "frontier" farming country, and increased agricultural production is bound up with the provision of roads and water supplies. The greater part of her agricultural production is for export, but growing industrialization and increasing population have led to reductions in the proportion of production exported. Before the war, 70 per cent of the wheat crop was exported, whereas in 1947–48 only 43 per cent went abroad. Australia's contribution to world food supplies will be a considerable factor during the next decade or so, but beyond that period it appears doubtful if there will be any large exportable surplus. During the last 20 years, population has risen by over 2½ millions, and continuation of immigration at 250,000 a year would bring the population to 12 millions by 1960. Development schemes for the large-scale raising of beef in the Northern Territories and of pork in Queensland are being undertaken, but it is as yet impossible to estimate how far those schemes will be successful in increasing exportable surpluses.

New Zealand is one of the most important food suppliers to world markets. Her small population of about 2 millions provides a large surplus of food which in contrast to Australia's is unlikely to be diminished in the near future by increased demands from the home market. Her livestock-producing industry of about ½ million tons of meat and ¼ million tons of butter and cheese has always been remarkably stable. More than 90 per cent of the major commodities were exported before the war, and though the proportion dropped during hostilities, when New Zealand was supplying the Allied Forces in the Pacific, and there was an acute shortage of refrigerated tonnage, production has increased steadily during the post-war period, and a rather larger proportion than pre-war is now exported.

The Middle East. In the Middle East, agricultural methods are in general very primitive, and a deep-rooted tendency to cling to extremely complicated customs of land tenure, causes severe hindrance to efforts to improve farming efficiency. Meat production receives scant attention as cattle are kept partly as draught animals, partly for their milk and hides, and partly, as in Africa, as an outward sign of their owners' social status. The Middle East is a net exporter of barley (chiefly from Iraq) and of rice (mainly from Egypt). Syria and Turkey are wheat exporters, but some wheat and maize is imported into Egypt, Lebanon and Israel. The Middle East is a natural granary, lying wholly in the wheat belt, and there is no apparent danger that the area will become a deficit area as regards food supplies. The under-developed countries of the Middle East can expand cultivation to feed their growing populations, but the "older" countries like Egypt may become net importers. There is a vast potential awaiting development, and Iraq in particular is exceptionally well placed with a fertile soil and abundant water supplies available from the Tigris and the Euphrates. Her rich stores of oil provide the means whereby the necessary development schemes can be financed to provide flood control, irrigation and the drainage necessary to prevent salting of the land from irrigation waters.

Africa. Africa is a sparsely populated country, and as far as the natives are concerned, a low income region. Broadly speaking, there are two kinds of agricultural production, (1) Cereals and root crops, which are mainly for local consumption and form the mainstay of the natives' diet, and (2) export crops, including oilseeds, sugar, coffee, cocoa, citrus fruits, tobacco, cotton and sisal. Despite war-time developments, native African dietary standards remain among the lowest in the world. As a whole, Africa is a comparatively empty continent with great potentialities for development, but taken as a whole it is the least well documented continent and only a fragmentary picture of the food and agricultural situation is possible.

In the Union of South Africa, wheat production doubled in the ten years before the war; at the same time maize production increased by about 55 per cent, but is liable to be severely affected in drought years. Meat was exported before the war from the Union and Southern Rhodesia, but Union meat exports have now ceased, and those from Rhodesia are likely to disappear before long. The chief reason is increased consumption per person and this is also the case with sugar and wheat. The Union now needs to import 40 per cent of its wheat and flour requirements, whereas before the war imports were needed only when the harvests were bad. Union maize exports were resumed for the first time since the war out of the record 1948 crop, but a consistent export surplus is unlikely.

India and the Far East. This region is predominantly rice-eating, and may be roughly divided into surplus and deficit rice areas. The former comprises Burma, French Indo-China and Thailand. The deficit countries are India, Ceylon, Malaya, Singapore, British North Borneo, Sarawak, Hong Kong, Indonesia, the Philippines and Japan, all of which normally import some part of their rice supplies (China and Pakistan are not normally large rice importers). Korea and Formosa in pre-war years exported substantial quantities of rice (almost entirely to Japan), and Korea, but for the war, would probably have resumed exports to Japan. Large quantities of other grains, particularly wheat, barley and millets, are produced in India, Pakistan, China and Japan.

All the rice-exporting countries suffered severely as a result of the war and their combined production fell from about 14 million tons of milled rice in 1925 and 17½ million tons in 1938 to a little over 9 million tons in 1945. By 1948 production had risen to 13 million tons, but only Thailand had reached the pre-war level of output. Little information is available about the production of other food crops in the Far East such as roots and other vegetables. These are, however, relatively less important, since grains of all kinds provide from 60 per cent to 70 per cent of the total calorie intake in most of the countries.

Generally speaking, the Far East with the exception of Japan and China is one of the most backward and inefficient farming areas of the world. About 21·6 cwt of milled rice are produced per acre in Japan and 14·6 in China, but in India and Pakistan only 6·6 cwt., in British North Borneo 3·4 cwt. and in the surplus producing areas of Burma, Thailand and French Indo-China, only 6 to 7 cwt. an acre are produced. Japan's wheat yield before the war was 15 cwt. an acre, but since the war, largely because of lack of fertilizers, it has only been 9 cwt. In China, the yield is about 9 cwt. per acre and in India and Pakistan only 5½ cwt.

The explanation of the low yields obtained in most countries of Asia is to be found in the small size of farms—three-quarters are of 3 acres or less—and the heavy rents which are charged. Cultivators are too poor to purchase even the most modest equipment, and primitive tools are employed in much the same way as has been done for centuries. In pre-war years, the rice-importing countries of Asia obtained all their requirements from other countries in Asia, but since the war rice has had to be imported from South America, the U.S., Australia and Egypt. At times, wheat, maize and sorghums have been imported owing to world shortage of rice. Wheat has had to be imported into Pakistan during the last year or so, though before the war this area exported wheat.

If the Far East—the most crowded region in the world—is to achieve similar standards of living to those of the Western hemisphere, it must almost inevitably import food from some of the less-densely populated regions. To do so, countries of the Far East need to produce export goods on a sufficient scale to finance the desired food imports, and at the present time they are finding this very difficult. Malaya with rubber and tin exports, and Indonesia and the Philippines with copra and palm oils can fairly readily obtain their necessary food imports, especially as their needs are small relative to those of other Far Eastern countries.

India in recent years has required to import some four million tons of grain annually, but her Government had hoped to be self-sufficient in food by 1951. This aim has not been achieved, and in 1951 a food crisis developed as a result of a series of misfortunes. Three years of bad harvests, accompanied by earthquakes, floods, droughts and epidemics, reduced food supplies so seriously that the country was faced with famine. Nevertheless India produced nearly 1 million extra tons of food in 1949–50 as compared with the previous year, mainly as a result of extended irrigation from numerous small works such as dams, channels and tube wells. Over 60,000 such wells were sunk in 1948. Wisely India is proceeding on the lines of numerous smaller schemes of improvement pursued simultaneously rather than on embarking on grandiose projects often so impressive on paper, but disappointing in practice. There is still a great deal to be done and India is dependent on imports of foodstuffs to the extent of 2 million tons of grain or more even in a good year.

Japan is also faced with the problem of paying for large

food imports, and is likely to seek markets wherever she can for her textiles and other goods in the near future; for Japan—like Britain—must export or die.

The growth of population in the Far East (except for China) is very considerable. In India and Pakistan, population increased by 83 millions between 1921 and 1941, and is at present growing by over 5 millions annually. Japan with 80 million inhabitants now has 10 millions more than in 1939, and there is an additional 1¼ million to be fed each year. China is the only large country in the area where a similar trend is not apparent, for in China population growth has been checked by famine, disease and war. In the Far East generally, populations are increasing rapidly, not as a result of any increase in the birth rate, but as a result of the lengthening of life, due to applications of modern science and medicine. Agriculture, which is very backward, is not keeping pace and science has not been applied, except in certain favoured areas, to increasing production. This backwardness is due largely to apathy, and to the fact that many millions live in areas remote from towns, to lack of education, and to the influence of the "cake of custom" which prevents individuals striking out on new, enterprising lines.

U.S.S.R. Before the First World War, Russia was a major producer and exporter of cereals; wheat exports averaging 4½ million tons per annum. Between the two wars, although production was expanded, domestic consumption increased and grain exports fell. Wheat exports amounted to only 0·6 million tons per annum in the 1934–38 period.

Since the end of the First World War the structure of Russian agriculture has been transformed. Large estates and primitive small holdings have given place to an economy based on large-scale State and Collective Farms equipped with a good supply of modern equipment. The process of transformation was slow, and it was not until 1929 that agriculture was integrated into the national economic plans. By 1938 some 26 million former small peasant holdings had been replaced by 3,960 State Farms and 242,000 Collectives which between them contained 96 per cent of the sown area.

Mechanization had by then made rapid progress and production of grains is estimated to have averaged 93 million tons. In addition, 10 million tons of grain were then being produced in those areas which have since been incorporated within the boundaries of the U.S.S.R. There has certainly been an increase in total food production since the introduction of collectivization, but this has so far done little more than keep pace with the increase in population and urbanization, especially as Russian agriculture suffered severely from the effects of the late war. Adequate statistical data is not available, and it is therefore difficult to assess the position in the U.S.S.R.

World Consumption Levels. The world food problem is neither homogeneous nor static, and there are great extremes in consumption levels as well as great differences in the efficiency of agricultural production. There is, for example, a marked contrast between the newly settled countries such as the U.S., Canada, Australia and New Zealand and the older countries, but even among those countries which have been long settled there is a marked contrast between Western Europe, with its highly efficient agriculture, its industry and extensive trade, and Far Eastern countries which have remained largely untouched by advances in European and American technology, both agricultural and industrial. The East, however, is now stirring and inevitably will demand higher food standards in the future.

Consumption level statistics are now published in the form of Food Balance Sheets by the Food and Agriculture Organization of the United Nations (F.A.O.) for some 70 countries of the world. The results are still tentative and the method needs further elaboration and refinement before the figures for various countries can be regarded as conclusive. This is especially true of countries where the statistical coverage is of a rudimentary nature. These facts are recognized by F.A.O., which itself has pointed out that the food balance sheets which it has prepared for many countries are still only rough approximations, and in order to assist governments in the construction of food balance sheets, a valuable handbook was prepared in

1949[1] and new food composition tables have been compiled for use in the preparation of food balance sheets in order to promote comparability in the presentation of food consumption data. The Handbook states that: "It is recognized that food balance sheets will continue to remain an imperfect tool in the examination and improvement of national food programmes until the range and accuracy of national statistics on food and agriculture have been greatly increased. It is hoped, however, that compilation by governments of their own food balance sheets will lead to considerable improvement both in national statistics and in balance-sheet technique." F.A.O. expressed the hope that by constructing food balance sheets, interest would be stimulated in the study of food consumption levels and diets and that as a result governments would use the information brought to light by this technique to plan their food production and trade programmes and to improve the nutritive value of the national food supply.

Within limitations, food balance sheets for any given period may be used, provided methods of calculation are comparable from one country to another, to compare the national average food supplies and the quantities of calories and nutrients available to the population as a whole in different countries. "In practice," says the Handbook, "the types and composition of foodstuffs produced, and the coverage and quality of statistics concerning them, vary so widely from country to country that strict comparability is difficult to attain; therefore, comparison of the food balance sheet for one country with that for another may be seriously misleading, unless due account is taken of such differences."

As complete accuracy is at present unobtainable and detailed figures might be misleading without unduly detailed explanations, the following table has been compiled from F.A.O. data in a form which is is hoped will afford a general picture of comparative consumption levels.

---

[1] *Handbook for the Preparation of Food Balance Sheets.* F.A.O. 1949.

Consumption Levels, 1948–49
Calories per person per day

Over 3,000	2,500–3,000	2000–2,500	Below 2,000
Argentina	Austria	Chile	Algeria
Australia	Belgium	Egypt	Burma
Canada	Cuba	Greece	Ceylon
Denmark	Czechoslovakia	Italy	India
Eire	Finland	Mexico	Japan
New Zealand	France	Peru	Morocco
Norway	Netherlands	Portugal	Tunisia
Sweden	Poland	Spain	
United Kingdom	Switzerland	Thailand	
U.S.A.	Turkey		
	Union of S. Africa		
	Uruguay		
	W. Germany		

The problem of raising world standards of diet is essentially a problem in the first place of improving the indigenous production of staple foods. Far and away the greatest proportion of food production throughout the world is for home consumption, and the proportion of the world's total production of staple foods that enters international trade is relatively small, amounting in the case of bread grains to about 17 per cent of total production and in that of coarse grains to about 6 per cent. With rice the proportion of the production which enters world trade was little more than 3½ per cent pre-war, while to-day it is even less, amounting to about 2 per cent.

For other commodities the proportion entering world trade varies from about 11 per cent in the case of meat to 27 per cent for oils and fats and 35 per cent for sugar. Even higher proportions of the plantation crops such as tea and coffee are grown for export.

The war led to considerable changes in the pattern of the diet of many countries, as for example, in Western Europe, where the proportion of calories derived from cereals and potatoes greatly increased.

The world position regarding rice, which is of the utmost

importance to the vast populations of the Far East, even though not all Far Eastern peoples are rice eaters, is less satisfactory than that of bread grains. Rice production—even before allowance is made for increased populations—is not yet back to the pre-war figure. Before the war, some 5½ million tons of rice entered international trade from Asiatic sources, nearly 5 millions of which went to India, China and Ceylon. By 1945 this had dwindled to a bare half-million tons—a measure of the devastating effect of the war on the food situation in the Far East. By the early months of 1948 a considerable recovery had been effected as a result of better harvests, and total exports of rice rose to 2½ or 3 million tons. The increased production has been maintained, and at the same time the Asiatic demand for wheat and flour which had been diverted from the common pool of international supplies, began to fall steadily.

The total volume of food produced in the world is now nearly the same as that produced before the war; the improvement being due to progress in rehabilitation of war-devastated areas, and to the continued high level of food production in certain countries whose territories were not affected by war operations.

In 1948, unusually good weather throughout the world and excellent harvests in North America enabled crop production *per caput* to attain pre-war levels, but in 1949 crop production declined to about 3 per cent below pre-war, though it was considerably above that of 1947. The main declines in 1949 as compared with 1948 were in coarse grains and potatoes; the decline in the former being mainly due to a fall in United States production from the previous year's record level. There was, however, an increase in world meat and milk production, and the output of oils and fats was slightly above the pre-war averages. In the Far East, excluding China, food production in 1949 was somewhat higher than in the previous year, especially in the deficit areas. The position is summarized in the following table of world production of the main foodstuffs and an analysis of food production by regions will be found in Table 31 of the Statistical Appendix.

11

Britain's Food Supplies

World Food Production. Million metric tons

	Pre-war	1948	1949
Bread grains	148·3	162·1	158·4
Coarse grains	196·5	245·1	228·8
Rice (paddy)	149·4	147·4	147·1
Sugar	26·1	30·4	30·7
Potatoes	158·8	164·9	143·3
Fats and Oils	23·4	24·4	24·5

Notes: (*a*) Fats and oils include vegetable, animal and marine. (*b*) U.S.S.R. excluded.

According to a report on the world situation by F.A.O., the year 1949–50 was a fairly good one. Although there was a slight decrease of volume of production of certain foodstuffs, the output of plant products was in general maintained or increased and this, together with the good harvest of 1948, had the effect of expanding the livestock industry. The level of food consumption per head per day was higher than in 1948–49 in about half the countries for which figures are available. In nearly all the remaining countries, the level was about the same. For the first time since the outbreak of the Second World War, fertilizers and agricultural machinery were freely available to all those producers who could afford to pay for them. Currency difficulties, however, prevented some countries from purchasing all the machinery they needed and shortage of dollars remained a serious problem in 1950. The report concludes that though the world production of food has shown some improvement, there is as yet no cause for over-confidence in the future nor must it lead to relaxation of effort. One bad harvest in a major producing area would mean the loss of the ground so painfully won in recent years.

In a later report on the year 1949–50, (F.A.O. Monthly Bulletin, March 1952) emphasis was placed on the deterioration in the world pattern of consumption. The Report states "not only has there been an appreciable decrease in average calorie supplies in the poorly fed regions of the world, but, what is equally disturbing, the large disparities which existed between the better and worse-fed nations before the war have conspicuously widened." In the following eighteen months it is admitted the position improved somewhat, but not sufficiently so to alter the general picture.

To improve the food supply of the world, the greatest step forward which could be taken would be to bring the efficiency of food production in the under-developed countries more nearly up to that of the more efficient. It is significant that the Food and Agriculture Committee of O.E.E.C. in its Interim Report issued at the end of 1949 was concerned with ways of improving the technical efficiency of European agriculture. Even European agriculture, immeasurably more efficient as it is than that of so many countries in the Far East, offers great scope for increased productivity. This Committee indeed estimated that the productivity of the 25 million hectares of Western Europe's grassland could be increased by 40 per cent, apart from improvements in haymaking and silage. It is also necessary to clear the way for an expanded world trade in agricultural products so that the surpluses of one part of the world may become available for deficit areas. The first and most important step, however, remains that of increasing agricultural efficiency in the under-developed countries themselves.

The world's standard of feeding could also be improved to an appreciable extent by the reduction of waste. F.A.O. has estimated that losses of bread grains and rice alone, through various forms of preventable waste, amount to some 33 million tons annually. Sir John Russell has pointed out that rats and mice destroy 2 million tons of food in England and Wales alone, and that a single rat is said to consume 50 lb. of grain a year and to spoil an additional 1½ cwt. Grass, which Sir John Russell describes as our most important and for long most neglected crop, when made into hay commonly loses 30 per cent or more of its valuable protein equivalent. The essentials in preventing waste are better storage and transport, improved sowing, harvesting and threshing facilities, and the education of housewives in the preparation of food. Soil erosion has been a serious factor in reducing food production, but it can be obviated by devices such as the planting of wind breaks, introduction of binding grasses, crop rotations, contour ploughing, and in general by correct utilization of land and water over the whole of the catchment area.

CHAPTER TWELVE

International Organizations

GLARING contrasts exist between the best fed and the worst fed nations of the world, and though this inequality is no new phenomenon, there is now a greater awareness of the problem, partly as a result of the growing feeling of unity throughout the world and partly because the facts have become better known through the publication of more detailed statistical and nutritional data. Everywhere, public opinion has been deeply impressed by the gravity and urgency of the problem.

Never before have so many schemes been drawn up to improve the lot of those nations whose nutritional standards fall below a tolerable minimum or so many plans made to bridge the gap between the potential world demand for food and the supply of agricultural produce. The problems to be solved are twofold. First, there is the need for improving indigenous production and this calls primarily for what has come to be known as "technical assistance". Second, there is the problem of local surpluses and the transference of these surpluses to nations whose own supplies are deficient. This is a problem involving physical transport, financing and, possibly also, changes in food consumption habits. The problems presented by local surpluses are not new, though frequently in the past the only solution attempted has been through restrictions on production which aimed at restoring or raising market prices. There has been a long succession of restrictive schemes, among which the best-known are the Greek Currant Retention Scheme, Coffee Valorization and the Wheat Pools. There have also been a number of international commodity agreements whereby exporting countries have agreed to restrict production to a quantity which could be sold at a remunerative price. Among these may be instanced the International Wheat Agreement of 1933 which lasted for one year only, and the more permanent Chadbourne Agreement on sugar production of 1931, which was followed by the International Sugar Agreement of 1937.

The fear of surpluses, or gluts as they used to be called, has not infrequently led producers to take a jaundiced view of the benefits of greater productivity, and this attitude is epitomized in the old rhyme of the Canadian prairies:

> "Here lies the body of Farmer Pete
> Who starved from growing too much wheat."

During the world depression, which occurred between the two world wars, stocks of cereals and coffee were actually burnt, or surpluses of other commodities were dumped into the sea in endeavours to raise prices to a level which would give adequate remuneration to the producers.

While the waste caused by the destruction of surpluses rightly shocks the world, and cannot be too strongly condemned, it must be remembered that the quantities involved are marginal, and the phrase so often quoted, "scarcity in the midst of plenty" is nonsense. There is no plenty. The real problems are those of increasing productivity and distributing local surpluses as and when they arise. Furthermore, surpluses and deficits may not match: for example a surplus of coffee in Brazil would not alleviate a shortage of rice in India. The dilemma which faces the world, however, is real enough, though its nature is often misunderstood, and it has been expressed vigorously by Norris Dodd, Director-General of F.A.O., in these words: "On one side of the gap stand consumers—many of them desperately hungry—eager to have more of the things they need, eager to earn more to pay for them as fast as they can. On the other side stand producers, afraid that if they produce as they can and would like, they will drown themselves in unsold surpluses."

Since the war, the nations of the world have inaugurated important and far-reaching schemes for improvement in the world's nutritional standards, which may be summed up in the motto of F.A.O. *"Fiat Panis."* Though much of the international endeavour in this sphere had its origin in the post-war period, when the world having sown the winds of war was reaping the whirlwinds of economic dislocation and devastation, its beginnings can be traced back to war-time organizations and indeed to the pre-war period. Great Britain as the world's greatest food importer has a special interest in all schemes for the improvement of international food supplies. Also, as a member of the British Commonwealth of Nations and the trustee for the Colonial Empire, she has special responsibilities in this field. In the following paragraphs, some account is given of various international organizations which aim at the improvement of the world's food supplies while in the following chapter an attempt will be made to describe the various schemes which have been developed within the Commonwealth and the Colonial Empire.

The Combined Food Board. A Combined Food Board was set up in 1942 by the United States and the United Kingdom for the purpose of making the best use of available foodstuffs and working out detailed plans for limited shipping facilities. Canada joined the Board in 1943 and it continued its activities after the war until it was replaced in 1946 by the International Emergency Food Council. In the transitional phase after the war, the Combined Food Board provided a ready means for formulating plans and considering recommendations regarding the production, procurement and distribution of food supplies available for export. In addition to the Combined Food Board, a London Food Council was also established, consisting of representatives of the United Kingdom, Australia, New Zealand, South Africa, India, Southern Rhodesia and the Colonies. This body worked in close co-operation with the Board and was responsible for control of the food exports and imports of the British Commonwealth (other than Canada) and of certain regions in the Eastern hemisphere such as the Middle East. Both the Board and the Council set up Commodity Committees for each of the major foodstuffs. These Commodity Committees met at frequent intervals to assess the current position and to make recommendations regarding the distribution of foodstuffs available for export where supplies fell short of the demand. After the end of the war membership of the Commodity Committees of the Combined Food Board was expanded to include representatives of the liberated countries and of exporting countries not previously parties to an agreed distribution of their produce. An U.N.R.R.A. representative attended meetings of the Committees of the Board dealing in foodstuffs in which that organization was interested in order to support the reasonable claims of countries for which it was responsible. Information regarding supplies, requirements, pre-war consumption, stocks and similar matters required for the preparation of recommendations was provided for the Committees by the governments concerned, and this co-operation enabled the Committees to be fully briefed regarding the current supply and demand position. The Board secured the co-ordination of purchases, prevented competitive buying and enabled allocations to be carried out effectively. Supplies were obtained from nearly 50 areas and were distributed to more than 70 territories. For some commodities such as tea, meat and sugar, arrangements were made through the Board for one government to undertake bulk purchase on behalf of all importing countries.

European Organization. When in 1945 the liberation of Europe was effected, the problem of reconstruction had to be faced and to facilitate this work an Emergency Economic Committee for Europe (E.E.C.E.) was set up, this being the first co-operative post-war organization to be established. As one of the most important problems facing the Committee was that of securing adequate food for a Europe on the verge of starvation, a special Food and Agricultural Sub-Committee was appointed, and this body continued in regular and frequent session for nearly two years, until its functions were taken over by other organizations.

About the same time another committee was also set up in London under the auspices of U.N.R.R.A. which came to be known as the Combined Working Party and consisted of representatives of the United States, the United Kingdom and the European Governments at that time established in London. The Combined Working Party undertook the assessment of the needs of European countries released from enemy occupation in relation to the supplies of food and other commodities available. In 1947, E.E.C.E. was wound up when the Economic Commission for Europe (E.C.E.) was established, and the activities of the E.E.C.E. Sub-committee on Food and Agriculture were transferred to the F.A.O. European Office which by then had been set up in Rome.

In 1947, the Organization of European Economic Co-operation (O.E.E.C.) was set up to represent the countries benefiting from Marshall Aid, and this body appointed a special Food and Agriculture Committee which has concerned itself with the problems of improving the agriculture and nutrition of European countries under the Marshall Plan.

Pflimlin Plan. Early in 1951 discussions took place on a plan suggested by Pierre Pflimlin, the French Minister of Agriculture, for the integration of European agricultural production on lines similar to those proposed under the Schuman Plan for coal and steel. The plan aims at the rationalization of European agricultural production by the gradual elimination of tariff barriers, quotas and subsidized production, though initially it is suggested consideration would be confined to the production and marketing of wheat, sugar, dairy produce and wine. Participating countries would put all their export production of these commodities into a common pool which would then be divided according to the needs of the participants. The difficulties of such a plan would be even greater than those of the Schuman Plan since it would have to incorporate control by a central authority over production, marketing and prices, and would have to devise means of co-ordinating production with demand. The advocates of the plan stress the need for an increased measure of self-sufficiency in Western Europe, and emphasize the necessity of saving dollar imports after Marshall Aid ends. It is doubtful, however, if the plan will meet with acceptance, as it would necessitate a complete change in traditional policies of balanced agriculture and submission to a supra-national authority by producers who do not take readily even to control by their own governments.

F.A.O. The Food and Agriculture Organization of the United Nations had its origin in May 1943, when delegates of 44 nations met in Hot Springs, Virginia, to consider food and agriculture in relation to President Roosevelt's assertion on the fundamental rights of mankind. The Conference set up an "Interim Commission" to work out plans for an organization dealing with food and agriculture which would (1) collect, interpret and disseminate information on these matters, (2) promote national and international action in this field, and (3) furnish technical assistance to governments in the fields of nutrition, food and agriculture. The Interim Commission in addition to setting out in some detail the functions of the new organization, presented five reports dealing respectively with nutrition, agriculture, forestry, fisheries and marketing, examining in detail the field of the work to be covered and making recommendations for the work which should be undertaken by the new organization.

Twenty countries indicated their readiness to accept the proposed constitution of the new body and the first conference of the Food and Agriculture Organization was held in October 1945 at Quebec, when Sir John Boyd Orr was appointed as the first Director-General of F.A.O. The next step was to assemble an expert international staff and to begin the first programme of work. F.A.O. had hardly started when the world was confronted with the food crisis of 1946, and a special meeting was called in Washington by the new organization in May 1946, which made recommendations to Governments as to the best use which could be made of the inadequate 1946 harvest, and suggested ways in which a larger harvest might be secured in 1947. A new and more comprehensive agency called the International Emergency Food Council (I.E.F.C.) was set up in 1946 to replace the Combined Food Board, and F.A.O. was entrusted with the task of providing statistics and information which would be required by I.E.F.C., including a quarterly appraisal of the world food situation. I.E.F.C., which was responsible for the allocation of scarce foodstuffs on the basis of need, continued in operation until 1949. A further conference of F.A.O. was held in Copenhagen in September 1946, at which the Director-General was asked to submit a report on the adequacy of international institutions "to meet long-term problems concerned with the production, distribution and consumption of food and agricultural products, including the risk of accumulated surpluses".

By 1946, the membership of F.A.O. was 47 nations, and by 1950 the number of co-operating nations had increased to 63. In the following year, the headquarters of the Organization was moved from Washington to Rome, after lengthy discussion as to the most suitable location.

F.A.O. Activities. F.A.O. collects information relating to food and agriculture, forestry and fisheries from all parts of the world, member governments undertaking to report periodically on the progress which they are making towards achieving the objectives laid down by the Organization. National F.A.O. Committees have been set up in many member countries for the purpose of maintaining touch with governmental and non-governmental agencies working in the fields of food and agriculture. The great masses of information received by F.A.O. at its headquarters are analysed and interpreted by a specialized staff, and numerous reports and appraisals of the world food situation have been published based on this data. In addition to this more academic side of its activities, F.A.O. renders technical and highly practical assistance to those countries which request its aid. At a conference held towards the end of 1949, special stress was laid on the need for the provision of technical assistance for economic development, a programme for which had been approved earlier by the United Nations General Assembly. In the Preface to the Report of the Fifth Session of the Conference of F.A.O. the Director-General (Norris E. Dodd), explained the function of F.A.O. in the implementation of this programme as follows: "F.A.O.'s part in this is to help nations to help themselves. No relief operations, no large-scale direct international programmes are contemplated. They would not work. The idea is to help nations—when they request aid—along the road to economic development, and to put them in a position where they can attract whatever outside investments may be needed. F.A.O.'s job would be to supply expert assistance and advice in analysing needs, training personnel, starting specific technical programmes, and helping organize demonstrations."

The initiation of this expanded programme of technical assistance is of great importance, since lack of skill and technical knowledge is one of the most significant differences between the under-developed countries and the more advanced nations of the world. As a report of the committee of F.A.O. has stated: "It is not a coincidence or because of unusually favourable weather that bumper crops have been reaped in recent years by the more developed countries of North America and Western Europe. There is a long-term tendency for agricultural yields to increase in those countries, and the explanation lies in the work of scientists and research workers."

In its May 1950 Report, the Council of F.A.O. stresses the value of utilizing pilot projects, when appropriate, whether for experiment or demonstration purposes. In due course, it believes, the results achieved would spread by themselves and much wider benefits would eventually be reaped than by other methods.

F.A.O. has also stressed that it cannot give direct help to small producers as the task would be impossible and basically unsound. Only their fellow-countrymen in general can have sufficient influence with small producers to persuade and help them.

President Truman's Fourth Point. In his inaugural address of 20 January 1949, President Truman called for a "bold new programme for making the benefits of our scientific advances and industrial progress available for the improvement and growth of under-developed areas." As this was the fourth point made in his address the programme has come to be known as such. Briefly the proposal was that the United States should make available its technical knowledge to the peoples living in under-developed areas who might then, by combining their own resources with American "know-how", be enabled to improve the conditions under which they live.

Technical assistance is to be supplemented by fostering capital investment on a joint basis in areas needing development.

Elaborating his theme, President Truman pointed out that "More than half the people of the world are living in conditions approaching misery. Their food is inadequate. They are victims of disease. Their economic life is primitive and stagnant. Their poverty is a handicap and a threat both to them and to the more prosperous areas. For the first time in history, humanity possesses the knowledge and the skill to relieve the suffering of these people."

Shortly after President Truman's inaugural address was delivered, the United States Government asked the Economic and Social Council of the United Nations to consider what the United Nations and the specialized international agencies could do along the lines suggested in the address. As a result, a programme of technical developments was prepared by the United Nations and its various specialized organizations including F.A.O., to which reference has been made in previous paragraphs. A parallel approach to the problem has been adopted by the United States Government, in which an expanded United Nations programme has been encouraged, and at the same time the United States Government is developing its own bilateral technical assistance activities. Discussing the desirability of this dual approach to the problem of developing under-developed areas, F. O. Wilcox (Chief of Staff of the U.S. Senate Committee on Foreign Relations) pointed out that there were cogent arguments in favour of the work being done by the United Nations and its agencies. "It is only natural," he said, "that some countries, fearful of imperialistic designs, prefer to receive assistance from the United Nations, with all the protective assurances that multilateral co-operation involves, rather than to deal on a bilateral basis with an individual state".

On the other hand, the United States already had a number of projects under way, and certain types of work can be better administered by a compact team from one country rather than by a group of experts from several countries. "But the most persuasive argument," he stated, "is the financial one. At the present time very few members of the United Nations are in a position to make substantial contributions toward extraordinary expenditures of this type. It is believed that the fifteen to twenty-five million dollars planned for the first year of the expanded programme is about all that can be raised on a voluntary basis. . . . The only practical alternative, therefore, is for us to shoulder a part of the burden bi-laterally, at least until the other members of the organization are in a sounder financial position."[1]

[1] *Annals of the American Academy of Political and Social Science*, March 1950. This volume contains a valuable symposium on all aspects of the Fourth Point Programme.

CHAPTER THIRTEEN

Development Schemes in the Commonwealth and Colonies

Introduction. The Commonwealth and Colonies make important contributions to Britain's food supplies, particularly as regards cereals, dairy produce, oils and fats and meat, as will be seen from Table 2 in the Statistical Appendix. During the war and post-war shortages, when Britain's need was greatest, they gave generous help even to the extent of imposing rationing on themselves in order to assist the Mother Country. To a considerable extent, the food-importing economy of Britain is complementary to those of the food-producing countries within the Commonwealth. It has, therefore, been found possible to negotiate many long-term contracts which have proved mutually advantageous, giving, on the one hand, security to the producers overseas and, on the other hand, assuring the British consumer of regular supplies. As the parties to these contracts are bound by ties of kinship and common endeavour, they are likely to prove more satisfactory than similar contracts negotiated with foreign powers.

Britain has special responsibilities towards the economic development of the Commonwealth countries and the colonies, particularly those in Asia and Africa where the ideological struggle with Communism has to be fought largely in terms of contributions towards material betterment. Much has already been done and more is being planned, though, as the hard-bought experience of the groundnut scheme and the Gambia poultry farms has shown, good intentions and the investment of capital are not enough. Development has to be related to natural advantages, climate, soil and many other physical factors. Mother Nature still has the last word; she can be cajoled and persuaded, but she will not be coerced or driven —not even by bulldozers and tractors.

The Colombo Plan. In January 1950, the Commonwealth

Foreign Ministers meeting at Colombo agreed that special attention should be given to those problems of Southern Asia which could not be solved by the countries of that area by themselves, but required help from other parts of the world. Following this agreement on general policy, the Commonwealth Consultative Committee on South and South-East Asia prepared a Report which was published in November 1950, under the title "The Colombo Plan for Co-operative Economic Development in South and South-East Asia."[1]

The Report is concerned with a region comprising India, Pakistan, Ceylon, the Federation of Malaya, Singapore, North Borneo, Sarawak, Brunei, Burma, Thailand, the Associate States of Cambodia, Laos and Viet-Nam, and Indonesia, and which has a population of 570 million people, making up one-quarter of the population of the world. "Despite the abundance of human resources, the considerable natural wealth of the area has not in the past been developed rapidly enough to ease the increasing pressure of population upon the land. There is, therefore, great poverty among millions and an unceasing struggle for existence." The countries in this region play an important part in world economy, as it is a major source of the food and raw materials consumed throughout the industrialized world. For example, before the war it provided more than three-quarters of world exports of tea, and one-third of the oils and fats. Traditionally, the area has had a large trading surplus with North America, and a deficit with the United Kingdom and Western Europe. The earning of a dollar surplus by South and South-East Asia was an important factor in enabling the United Kingdom and Western Europe to finance their own dollar deficits before the War. These dollar earnings are an important element in the world's multilateral trading system.

"The conception of the Commonwealth countries' approach to the problem is that a fresh impetus should be given to economic development in South and South-East Asia, in order to increase production, raise standards of living, and thus enlarge the volume of trade around the world from which

[1] Cmd. 8080.

all countries may benefit. It is because this is a world problem of the first magnitude and not a purely national or regional one, that the Commonwealth Governments have framed this Report for the world's consideration."[1]

The Report emphasizes that the central problem of the region has been, and still is, the supply of food. The impact of war and post-war unrest has had most serious results on food supplies and widespread starvation has only been averted with difficulty.

Development Programmes, which are described in some detail in the Report, have been prepared by India, Pakistan, Ceylon and the Federation of Malaya, Singapore, North Borneo and Sarawak.. These were scheduled to begin in July 1951, and cover a period of six years. An outlay of £1,868 million is envisaged of which 34 per cent is for transport and communications, 32 per cent for agriculture, including river valley development schemes, 18 per cent for housing, health and education, and 10 per cent for industry, fuel and power. Among the results expected to be achieved from these plans are an increase of 13 million acres of land under cultivation and an increase of the same acreage of irrigated land. It is hoped to increase production of food grains by 10 per cent.

Commenting on the programmes, the Report concludes that they have been framed on a realistic basis, and that they are designed to provide the foundations for future progress rather than early dramatic results. Two main limitations on the possibility of implementing the programmes are discussed in some detail, namely the shortage of trained men and the shortage of capital, both internal and external. The latter shortage is probably the more serious and the present situation is in the nature of a vicious circle. Economic development is prevented by lack of savings and saving does not take place because of insufficient development. A large initial stimulus is therefore required in the form of foreign investment. To provide technical assistance, a Council for Technical Co-operation has been established, composed of representatives

[1] Cmd. 8080. Page 3.

12

from each of the participating Governments, assisted by a Bureau with headquarters in Colombo.

The Overseas Food Corporation. World food shortages in 1946 gave rise to serious concern in Britain about the prospects of obtaining adequate food supplies, and attention was turned to the possibilities of developing groundnut cultivation in East and Central Africa. To investigate the possibilities, a mission visited Tanganyika and other African territories in 1946 and a plan based on the recommendations of this mission was prepared which provided for the cultivation of over 3 million acres of bushland. It was estimated that for a capital expenditure of £24 million, over half-a-million tons of groundnuts could thus be supplied annually to Britain. In the White Paper which outlined the plan, it was suggested that "the most suitable and efficient instrument for the management of an undertaking of this kind is a Government-owned and financed Corporation created by Statute with clearly defined powers and duties and with its own separate organization and a responsible Board of Directors answerable to the Government but with the fullest scope for initiative."[1] Time, however, was felt to be pressing and in order to get the project started quickly, management of the scheme in its initial stages was entrusted to the United Africa Company, Ltd. In the meantime the Overseas Resources Development Act, 1948 was passed through Parliament and under this Act an Overseas Food Corporation was immediately set up and took over control of the groundnut scheme early in 1948. The Corporation also became responsible for a number of smaller projects, including the Queensland scheme for pig-rearing.

Though the dual objectives of the groundnut scheme, namely the economic development of Africa and the supply of much-needed food to Britain, were in themselves excellent, the methods pursued were over-ambitious and grandiose, with the result that the scheme has resulted in a loss of £36½ million. It was launched as though it were a gigantic military operation, and indeed military metaphors constantly recurred

[1] *A Plan for the Mechanized Production of Groundnuts in East and Central Africa.* Cmd. 7030. Page 8.

in subsequent reports on its progress or in extenuation of its lack of progress. No pilot investigations were considered necessary, and it thus departed from its own conception of a military operation, which would normally be preceded by small raids and trials of strength. It appears to have been thought by its sponsors that if only enough machines were used and sufficient capital applied, success could not fail to be achieved. The story of the groundnut failure is well-known and does not need any detailed revpition here. Briefly, the sequence of events was that the Goetrnment was eventually forced, in November 1949, by ever-increasing losses to reduce the original plan for cultivating 3 million acres to a mere 600,000 acres. Even this drastic pruning was not sufficient, and in 1951 the scheme became nothing more than an experimental development project for the clearance of 210,000 acres by 1954. At the same time, control was transferred from the Minister of Food to the Secretary of State for the Colonies. The tractor force employed was to be drastically reduced in favour of the slower but cheaper clearing of land by hand labour. The epitaph of the original scheme was written in a White Paper[1] in these words: "The revised programme submitted by the Overseas Corporation involves a radical change in the whole conception of the scheme. The original aim was to increase production of oils and fats to meet a world shortage which was and still is expected to persist. It was hoped that within a comparatively short time the scheme would make a substantial contribution to world supplies. This hope has not been fulfilled, and while the possibility remains that in time Tanganyika may contribute to world oils and fat supplies, the Corporation's proposals show that too much has yet to be learned about methods of land clearing and large-scale mechanized agriculture in Tanganyika to give any grounds for supposing that rapid development over wide areas is at present practicable."

The Overseas Food Corporation has also been responsible through an associated corporation, the Queensland British Food Corporation, for the much less ambitious, but more

[1] *The Future of the Overseas Food Corporation.* Cmd. 8125. Page 5.

promising, Queensland scheme for the production of pig-meat. This project originated through a proposal from the Queensland Government for the production of groundnuts. An investigation early in 1948 showed that the conditions were not favourable for this crop and the original proposal was re-placed by a project for growing sorghum on a series of over-grazed sheep pastures with the aim of feeding the grain to pigs which, along with part of the grain grown, would be exported to Britain.

Colonial Development Corporation. This body was set up in February 1948 under the provisions of the Overseas Resources Development Act and was authorized to raise capital up to the amount of £100 million under the authority of the Secre-tary of State for the Colonies for the purpose of assisting de-velopment schemes in the British Colonies. Each scheme has to be sanctioned by the Secretary of State for the Colonies, and the Corporation has been charged with the financial responsibility of securing that their revenues are not less than that required to meet all sums properly chargeable to their revenues account, taking one year with another.

Hundreds of schemes have already been examined by the Corporation, and of these 46 had been approved and were in operation by the end of 1950. Of these projects, as might be expected, 16 are in the main agricultural, 4 are concerned with animal products and 6 relate to fisheries. Among the projects now being undertaken may be mentioned the Bahamas Development Undertaking, the British Honduras Fruit Com-pany, the Swaziland Irrigation Scheme and the Bechuanaland Cattle Ranch. The Swaziland scheme, which is an 18-year development project for some 16,000 square miles, aims at finding good soil and sufficient water which, with irrigation, will provide 80,000 acres suitable for high-crop cultivation. The Nigerian Agricultural Project, approved in 1949, is designed to integrate local agricultural skill with modern farming methods and mechanical assistance. In this enterprise the Government of Nigeria and the Corporation have an equal financial interest. The minimum and economically effective operations are to be done by machinery, but settler and experimental labour will do as much work as is practicable under skilled agricultural supervision. Settlers will have 36 acres each, of which, in any year, 12 acres will be fallow or sown to grass. With the exception of the Gambia Poultry and River Farms scheme, which proved so disappointing and futile, the work of the Colonial Development Corporation has on the whole been characterized by careful assessment of the various projects submitted to it. Aid has only been given after a careful balance of the worth of the particular scheme and the need of the Colony for economic development has been made. The Gambia scheme was a repetition on a smaller scale of the precipitate and expensive venture in groundnut production. When the project was launched in 1948, the intention was to clear 10,000 acres of bush, to set up sawmills to produce timber for sale and to grow enough sorghum and other crops to feed a laying flock of 200,000 poultry, yielding 20 million eggs and 1 million pounds of dressed poultry a year. These aims, however, were never achieved, and by 1951 the scheme had run into grave difficulties; 30,000 birds died from disease in the summer of 1950, and sufficient foodstuffs could not be grown to feed the proposed number of hens. Some £825,000 had been spent, and a substantial amount of this has had to be written off. The lesson to be learnt from the Gambia failure is the same as that taught by the groundnuts failure, namely that large-scale mechanized conversion of bush into farmland is not merely a matter of tractors and bulldozers. The soil, climate and the limitations on agriculture in the tropics have to be carefully studied and time has to be allowed for experiments to be made.

CHAPTER FOURTEEN

Prospects for the Future

THOUGH long-term economic prophecy is a dangerous field in which to speculate, our account of Britain's food supplies would be incomplete and unsatisfactory without some assessment of future prospects. In this connection, the continued shortages of food since the war, and the constant difficulties which have had to be faced by Britain in obtaining adequate supplies of food raise a fundamental question. Have conditions so far changed in the second half of the twentieth century that Britain must resign herself to the inadequate standards which have been all that she has been able to maintain since the war, or worse still, will it be necessary to reduce standards of living in the future? Britain is a highly industrialized nation of some 50 million inhabitants, four-fifths of whom live in urban areas. Home agriculture cannot be expanded sufficiently to provide enough food for the people of these islands; indeed to raise home production to anything much over half the total requirements would probably involve disproportionate cost. Britain must continue therefore to depend on other countries for the major part of her food requirements. The possibility of obtaining adequate supplies of food from overseas depends, apart from any new supply areas which may be developed, on there being a continued surplus of production over requirements in areas which in the past have produced for export and on this country being able to purchase the surplus in competition with other buyers. Behind this question of the availability of surpluses, there looms a problem which has aroused violent controversies and not a little prejudice, namely the problem of the relative growth of world population and food supplies.

Population pressure on resources. During recent years, several books have appeared dealing with population questions in which alarming prospects for mankind are depicted unless population growth is quickly checked. There was a similar though more dialectical discussion, a few years after the end of the First World War, during which one writer summed up the genesis of the controversy by a reference to the Malthusian Devil having been unchained on the banks of the Cam. To-day, Malthusianism has indeed returned with a vengeance, and some writers have despaired of any attempts to increase food production because they argue that a "devastating torrent of births" will result so that the net effect will only be a greater population to eat the extra food. Others, in the fashionable strain of realistic pessimism current to-day, argue that not only is population increasing disproportionately, but that also the power to produce food is dwindling owing to soil erosion, salting up of irrigated lands, "wheat mining" and other evils. Terrifying pictures are thus presented to us of mankind brought to the brink of starvation through the combined effects of wasted resources and the growth of population. The whole subject of world population is one highly charged with emotion and as positions are often held with passionate fervour, the real nature of the problem has tended to be obscured. It is not in fact as sharp and clear-cut as many would have us believe because, as was shown in a previous chapter, there are great regional differences in agricultural production and in population growth.

Overall, the population of the world increased by slightly less than one per cent per annum between 1900 and 1950 but the increase was uneven, being about two per cent in the Near East, Latin America and Africa; somewhat over one per cent in the Far East but less than one per cent in Europe. Some writers assert that the rate of growth in world population is increasing and that the population of the world will double itself within the next fifty years or so. Generalization, however, is unsafe because many complex factors are involved and we do not really know very much about the influences which affect the fertility rate, or about the great secular trends of population growth or decline which manifest themselves throughout the ages or in different regions of the world. In so far as it is safe to generalize, it would seem that where a marked increase in population occurs, it is due not so much to any increase in the birth rate as to a decrease in the death rate. This would appear to be true of the Far East where the greatest absolute increase in population has taken place during recent years. Reference to the United Nations Statistical Yearbook will show that there has been a decline in the crude birth rate in practically all the countries of that region between 1930 and 1950.

Improvements in sanitation and advances in the science and practice of preventive medicine have been largely responsible for decreases in the death rate, but these lead in time to higher standards of living. Increased industrialization in time also may be expected to bring about a slowing down in the growth of population as settled urban populations nowadays tend to increase more slowly than rural populations. Further as the death rate falls, it becomes harder to effect significant reductions. Once standards of living have been improved, population tends to become stabilized and the real crux of the population problem would appear to lie in the period during which death rates are falling but before stabilization has been achieved. During this period, the problem is to increase food production in those countries where population growth is greatest by an amount more than the 2 or 3 per cent per annum by which their population is growing. The necessary increases must come, as was stressed in an earlier chapter, in the main from the domestic production of the countries concerned. The difficulties are immense and must not be minimized, but technically it would not appear to be impossible to raise production sufficiently to bridge the gap before populations stabilized themselves.

The under-developed and backward countries start from a very low level of agricultural efficiency, and therefore the possibilities of technical improvement are considerable. According to a United Nations report on "Land Reform", output per person in agriculture in North America is approximately $2\frac{1}{2}$ tons, in Asia it is less than one-quarter of a ton and in Africa one-eighth of a ton. Technical assistance is now being provided by the more advanced countries through F.A.O., Point Four Programmes and other agencies, and it is in this direction that most hope lies for a solution. Increased production depends, however, not only on a transformation of immemorial agricultural practices; it is also necessary to transform cultural patterns and social organizations. The United Nations Report mentioned above stresses this aspect of the problem, pointing out that it is not sufficient to effect improvements in agricultural techniques and organization; the agrarian structure itself generally needs to be reformed at the same time.[1]

While no final answer can be given to the problem of world population and food resources because the imponderables are so numerous and our knowledge of the secular trends of population in relation to institutional frameworks and cultural patterns is very scanty, Britain's problems are of a more concrete kind, and therefore more easily evaluated.

Britain's Prospects for the Future. There is no question in Britain of any rapid increase in population, and the problems are concerned with possibilities of increased home production of food and the maintenance of adequate food imports. If Britain has the means to pay, she can obtain the food she requires because the surplus food-producing areas are on the whole not those where population pressure is greatest. Higher prices, however, will probably have to be paid to overseas producers. Conditions have altered greatly since the nineteen-thirties when Britain obtained her food very cheaply, and a change in the terms of trade since then has taken place against Britain. Former agrarian countries are now becoming industrialized, and all their eggs are no longer in one basket. World demand for food will probably continue to increase as other countries raise their standards of living and develop exports to pay for increased food imports. Britain, therefore, must set herself to produce those goods and services which other nations want and at a price and in the form which are attractive to the overseas buyer.

[1] *Land Reform. Defects in Agrarian Structure and Obstacles to Economic Development*, 1951.

Britain's economy since the end of the war has been tightly stretched and when in 1951 she embarked on a policy of re-armament, her ability to pay for food imports was markedly diminished. The difficulties which have had to be faced for example in obtaining meat supplies during recent years are symptomatic of Britain's general problem of securing essential food imports. Before 1939, she dominated world food markets; paying the piper she called the tune, but since the end of the war, she has been struggling with balance of payment diffi-culties and passing from crisis to crisis while areas formerly supplying her with meat have been finding alternative markets. Meat shortages during 1951 and 1952 reflected lack of stocks, which in part at least were due to balance of payment diffi-culties, and lack of response on the part of overseas producers to Britain's demand for food at the prices which she was pre-pared to pay. In the Argentine, more and more meat was being consumed at home and population has been rising faster than the number of cattle, while in Australia local consumption was also increasing. World re-armament and rising prices of raw materials also threw, for the time at least, the balance of advantage in favour of producing industrial crops such as cotton or wool rather than food crops for Britain. At the same time, home production of meat in Britain was restricted by lack of imported animal feedingstuffs, which brings us back once again to lack of the means of payments for imports. Similar though not so acute difficulties have had to be faced in con-nection with other foodstuffs especially those such as dairy produce which depend on grass and labour. It would seem inevitable that in the future a greater proportion of the national income will have to go to food than in the past, and as has so often been stressed, any increase in the standard of living of the people of this country depends on an all-round increase in productivity. If this cannot be achieved, then in the words used by Adam Smith in another connection, Britain will have to "endeavour to accommodate her future views and designs to the real mediocrity of her circumstances."

STATISTICAL APPENDIX

(Note. Pre-war period is taken as average of the years 1934–38.)

TABLE I

POPULATION OF THE UNITED KINGDOM. MILLIONS

Census Figures	England and Wales	Scotland	N. Ireland[1]	United Kingdom
1821	12·0	2·1	1·4	15·5
1831	13·9	2·4	1·6	17·8
1841	15·9	2·6	1·6	20·2
1851	17·9	2·9	1·4	22·3
1861	20·1	3·1	1·4	24·5
1871	22·7	3·4	1·4	27·4
1881	26·0	3·7	1·3	31·0
1891	29·0	4·0	1·2	34·3
1901	32·5	4·5	1·2	38·2
1911	36·1	4·8	1·3	42·1
1921	37·9	4·9	1·3	44·0
1931	40·0	4·8	1·2	46·0
1941[2]	41·7	5·1	1·3	48·2
1951	43·7	5·1	1·4	50·2

Notes. [1] The figures throughout refer to the area which is now Northern Ireland.
[2] Estimate.
As the figures have been rounded to the nearest hundred thousand, the totals for the United Kingdom do not necessarily correspond exactly to the addition of the three columns.

TABLE 2

THE CHANGE IN SOURCES OF BRITAIN'S FOOD IMPORTS

	Pre-war		1944		1948	
Wheat and Flour	Canada	40%	Canada	82%	Canada	78%
	Australia	24%	Argentina	12%	Australia	20%
	Argentina	15%				
Meat (including bacon)	Argentina	33%	Argentina	34%	New Zealand	34%
	New Zealand	18%	U.S.A.	22%	Argentina	31%
	Australia	14%	Canada	21%	Australia	16%
	Denmark	13%	New Zealand	11%	Canada	11%
Oils and Fats	British West Africa	19%	British West Africa	31%	British West Africa	50%
	India	14%	U.S.A.	17%	Argentina	14%
			India	14%		
			Argentina	12%		
Sugar	Cuba and San Domingo	37%	Cuba and San Domingo	79%	Cuba and San Domingo	53%
	Australia	15%	British West Indies and British Guiana	13%	British West Indies	18%
	Mauritius	11%			Australia	10%
	British West Indies and British Guiana	11%				
Butter, Cheese and all types of Canned Milk	New Zealand	32%	U.S.A.	47%	New Zealand	51%
	Denmark	17%	New Zealand	33%	Australia	20%
	Netherlands	15%			Denmark	14%
	Australia	14%				
Eggs (including processed eggs)	China	29%	U.S.A.	80%	Canada	32%
	Denmark	26%	Canada	10%	Denmark	18%
	Netherlands	11%			Australia	16%
					China	12%
Citrus Fruit	Spain	29%	Spain	56%	Palestine	44%
	Palestine	28%	Palestine	17%	Spain	20%
	S. Africa	13%	S. Africa	14%	S. Africa	16%
	Brazil	11%	Sicily/Italy	12%	Sicily/Italy	10%
Canned Fruit	U.S.A.	51%	U.S.A.	100%		
	Australia	14%			S. Africa	13%
	Straits Settlements	11%			Australia	83%

BRITISH AGRICULTURE

TABLE 3

UNITED KINGDOM LIVESTOCK POPULATION (AT JUNE CENSUS)

Million head

	1939	1940	1941	1942	1943	1944	1945	1946	1947	1948	1949	1950	1951
Cattle	8·9	9·1	8·9	9·1	9·3	9·5	9·6	9·6	9·6	9·8	10·2	10·6	10·5
Sheep	26·9	26·3	22·3	21·5	20·4	20·1	20·2	20·4	16·7	18·2	19·5	20·4	20·0
Pigs	4·4	4·1	2·6	2·1	1·8	1·9	2·2	2·0	1·6	2·2	2·8	3·0	3·9
Poultry	74	71	62	58	51	55	62	67	70	85	95	96	94

TABLE 4

CROP PRODUCTION IN THE U.K.

Million tons

	1939	1940	1941	1942	1943	1944	1945	1946	1947	1948	1949	1950	1951
Wheat	1·6	1·6	2·0	2·6	3·4	3·1	2·2	2·0	1·7	2·4	2·2	2·6	2·2
Oats	2·0	2·9	3·2	3·6	3·1	3·0	3·2	2·9	2·5	3·0	3·0	2·7	2·5
Other grains	1·0	1·3	1·6	1·9	2·0	2·2	2·5	2·3	2·0	2·6	2·8	2·5	2·6
Potatoes	5·2	6·4	8·0	9·4	9·8	9·1	9·8	10·2	7·8	11·8	9·0	9·5	8·0
Sugar Beet	3·5	3·2	3·2	3·9	3·8	3·3	3·9	4·5	3·0	4·3	4·0	5·2	4·6
Fodder crops¹	14·3	15·1	17·3	18·8	17·0	17·9	19·0	17·4	13·6	15·8	14·6	15·8	15·8
Fruit	0·8	0·6	0·3	0·7	0·7	0·7	0·5	0·7	1·0	0·8	0·9	0·7	1·0
Vegetables	2·4	2·6	2·9	3·7	3·1	3·4	3·2	3·0	2·7	3·4	2·3	3·1	2·4
Hay	7·8	7·0	6·6	6·7	6·7	5·7	7·2	6·8	7·2	7·2	7·5	7·3	

Sources. *Agricultural Statistics. United Kingdom, Part II. Output and Utilization of Farm Produce. Statistical Digests.*
¹ Turnips, swedes, mangolds, beans and peas.

TABLE 5

HOME-PRODUCED FOOD. CALORIES PER HEAD PER DAY

Year	Calories		
	Total Home and imported	From Home-produced food	Percentage Home-produced
Pre-war	3,000	920	31
1940	2,800	920	33
1941	2,820	870	31
1942	2,870	1,090	38
1943	2,860	1,230	43
1944	3,010	1,260	42
1945	2,930	1,200	41
1946	2,880	1,120	39
1947	2,880	1,090	38
1947-8	2,860	990	35
1948-9	2,960	1,170	40
1949-50	3,010	1,160	39

Note. The low home production figure for 1947 can be largely accounted for by a poor potato harvest. Prolonged wintry conditions early in 1947 and floods in some of the most productive areas had an adverse effect on agricultural production generally.

TABLE 6

LEVELS OF AGRICULTURAL PRODUCTION

(Pre-war = 100)

	Pre-war	1943–44	1946–47	Target for 1951–52
Wheat	100	209	119	160
Barley	100	215	257	279
Oats	100	158	150	156
Potatoes	100	202	209	158
Sugar Beet	100	137	165 (a)	131
Milk	100	101	107	123
Eggs	100	66	84	152
Beef and veal	100	83	93	110
Mutton and lamb	100	77	70	77
Pig meat	100	37	32	92

(a) There was an exceptionally high yield from sugar beet in this year.

TABLE 7

AGRICULTURAL PRODUCTION IN THE UNITED KINGDOM

	average 1936–39	1947–48	1948–49	1949–50	1950–51 estimate	1951–52 forecast
Acreage (Thousand acres)						
Bread grains	1,872	2,198	2,340	2,027	2,550	2,050
Other grains	3,429	5,866	6,016	5,992	5,721	5,700
Potatoes	723	1,330	1,548	1,308	1,235	1,220
Sugar beet	335	395	413	421	429	430
Production (Thousand tons)						
Bread grains	1,661	1,689	2,408	2,258	2,576	2,160
Other grains	2,781	4,514	5,508	5,770	4,910	5,083
Potatoes	4,873	7,766	11,798	9,035	9,637	8,540
Sugar beet	2,741	2,960	4,319	3,962	5,209	3,956
Production (Per cent of pre-war)						
Milk	100	109	123	129	135	139
Eggs	100	90	105	118	130	131
Beef and veal	100	82	88	102	104	109
Mutton and lamb	100	56	67	75	77	83
Pig meat	100	29	50	71	73	92

Source. *Economic Surveys, 1949 and 1951.*

TABLE 8

LANDINGS OF FISH OF BRITISH TAKING (LANDED WEIGHT) AND IMPORTED FISH

Thousand tons

	1938	1939	1940	1941	1942	1943	1944	1945	1946	1947
England and Wales	777	572	178	125	158	159	172	300	633	695
Scotland	269	213	136	120	147	150	152	192	268	299
Imported Fresh or Frozen	82	98	164	145	162	176	209	229	203	214
Canned Excludes shell fish	77	85	98	80	136	149	63	39	79	79

FOOD CONSUMPTION

TABLE 9

CONSUMPTION PER HEAD PER DAY
PERCENTAGE OF PRE-WAR

Year	Calories	Proteins			Fats All sources	Carbo-hydrates
		Animal	Vegetable	Total		
Pre-war	100	100	100	100	100	100
1940	93	90	109	98	93	93
1941	94	84	126	103	87	97
1942	96	94	124	108	91	96
1943	95	93	122	107	89	98
1944	100	97	123	109	95	102
1945	98	99	127	112	89	102

Source. Cmd. 7842.

TABLE 10

ANNUAL CONSUMPTION
OF MAIN FOODS IN LB. PER HEAD IN THE U.K.

THE WAR YEARS

	Pre-war	1940	1941	1942	1943	1944	1945
Dairy Produce (milk solids)	38·3	38·2	40·7	48·6	50·0	49·0	49·8
Meat (edible weight)	109·6	98·8	85·6	89·6	86·4	96·1	86·6
Fish (edible weight)	26·7	17·1	15·5	16·7	18·3	20·3	24·6
Eggs (fresh egg equivalent)	28·6	22·4	19·2	21·0	22·1	23·2	26·1
Oils and fats (fat content)	45·3	41·2	39·9	39·6	37·9	39·0	37·0
Potatoes	176·0	166·4	188·2	224·9	248·8	274·6	260·2
Grain Products	210·1	225·8	257·2	245·7	248·9	252·8	258·0
Sugar and syrups (sugar content)	109·9	77·6	70·9	·72·1	71·6	75·7	74·1
Vegetables	107·5	98·5	109·1	119·6	117·1	124·8	127·1
Fruit and tomatoes (fresh equivalent)	141·4	108·0	59·7	94·2	77·9	93·6	90·9
Tea	9·3	8·6	8·1	8·2	7·0	7·4	8·2

Sources. *Food Consumption Levels in United Kingdom.* Cmd. 7842 and Ministry of Food.

TABLE 11

ANNUAL CONSUMPTION
OF MAIN FOODS IN LB. PER HEAD IN THE U.K.
THE POST-WAR YEARS

	Pre-war	1946	1947	1948	1949
Dairy Produce (milk solids)	38·3	49·4	48·7	49·1	52·4
Meat (edible weight)	109·6	89·9	82·0	73·8	74·6
Fish (edible weight)	26·7	31·0	31·8	31·8	28·0
Eggs (fresh egg equivalent)	28·6	21·9	20·9	21·3	28·4
Oils and Fats	45·3	34·7	33·9	38·1	44·3
Potatoes	176·0	282·0	284·1	237·2	255·5
Grain Products	210·1	237·8	240·2	249·4	238·0
Sugar and syrups (sugar content)	109·9	79·1	85·0	85·3	91·1
Vegetables	107·5	115·8	114·0	117·2	104·5
Fruit and Tomatoes (fresh equivalent)	141·4	109·8	132·4	137·4	130·6
Tea	9·3	8·8	8·5	8·0	8·1

Sources. *Food Consumption Levels in United Kingdom.* Cmd. 7842 and Ministry of Food.

TABLE 12

NUTRIENT EQUIVALENT OF SUPPLIES PER HEAD PER DAY
MOVING INTO CIVILIAN CONSUMPTION
IN THE UNITED KINGDOM

THE WAR YEARS

	Pre-war	1940	1941	1942	1943	1944	1945
Proteins, animal gm.	43·2	38·3	35·7	40·3	39·8	41·4	42·1
,, vegetable,,	37·2	40·4	46·7	46·3	45·5	45·7	47·2
,, total ,,	80·4	78·7	82·4	86·6	85·3	87·1	89·3
Fat (from all sources) ,,	130·7	120·7	113·4	118·9	115·3	124·0	116·0
Carbohydrates ,,	377·3	350·1	367·5	363·8	370·0	386·3	383·2
Calories	3,000	2,800	2,820	2,870	2,860	3,010	2,930

Sources. *Food Consumption Levels in United Kingdom.* Cmd. 7842, and Ministry of Food.

TABLE 13

NUTRIENT EQUIVALENT OF SUPPLIES PER HEAD PER DAY
MOVING INTO CIVILIAN CONSUMPTION
IN THE UNITED KINGDOM

THE POST-WAR YEARS

		Pre-war	1946	1947	1948	1949
Proteins, animal	gm.	43·2	44·3	41·7	41·1	42·9
,, vegetable	,,	37·2	46·0	47·7	46·4	45·8
,, total	,,	80·4	90·3	88·1	87·5	88·7
Fat (from all sources)	,,	130·7	112·0	108·2	107·6	119·4
Carbohydrates	,,	377·3	376·8	391·2	393·0	395·6
Calories		3,000	2,880	2,900	2,890	3,010

Sources. *Food Consumption Levels in United Kingdom.* Cmd. 7842 and Ministry
of Food.

TABLE 14

NUTRIENT EQUIVALENTS OF SUPPLIES PER HEAD PER DAY

		Pre-war	1941	1948
Calcium	mg.	695	698	1,199
Iron	mg.	12·6	12·9	15·8
Vitamin A	i.u.	4,042	3,604	4,145
Ascorbic Acid	mg.	96	81	109
Vitamin B1	mg.	1·2	1·5	1·8
Riboflavin	mg.	1·6	1·6	2·0
Nicotinic Acid	mg.	13·4	13·0	14·3

Sources. *Food Consumption Levels in United Kingdom.* Cmd. 7842 and Ministry
of Food.

MINISTRY OF FOOD HOUSEHOLD FOOD SURVEY

TABLE 15

CONSUMPTION OF CERTAIN FOODS IN THE HOME—URBAN WORKING CLASS HOUSEHOLDS

(in oz. per head per week unless otherwise stated)

Food	1942	1943	1944	1945	1946	1947 (b)	1948 (c)	1949
Bread and Flour	67·0	66·6	67·0	68·0	66·0	67·9	71·5	68·0
Meat	26·3	26·2	28·3	26·4	26·6	25·5	23·0	22·7
Butter and Margarine	6·1	6·2	6·3	6·3	6·3	6·2	7·1	7·7
Milk (liquid)　(a) pts.	3·5	3·9	4·0	4·1	4·0	4·0	4·1	4·4
Cheese	3·6	3·1	2·6	2·5	2·5	2·3	1·9	2·2
Sugar	8·4	8·7	9·1	9·1	9·6	10·2	10·5	10·9
Eggs (inc. dried equiv. eggs)	1·4	2·2	2·9	3·0	2·5	2·3	2·3	2·9
Potatoes (inc. chips)	68·5	71·2	71·3	68·5	73·8	70·9	66·0	68·9
Other Vegetables	31·4	34·5	37·3	36·4	34·5	30·8	32·7	31·0
Fruit	12·0	12·8	14·0	15·9	15·7	21·7	22·8	22·4
Fish	6·6	6·5	7·6	9·2	10·6	9·6	9·8	8·4

(a) Includes school milk except in 1942
(b) Average for January-September
(c) Average for year excluding February and March

TABLE 16

FOOD EXPENDITURE IN THE HOME—URBAN WORKING CLASS HOUSEHOLDS

(per head per week in pence)

Food	1937–38	1942	1943	1944	1945	1946	1947 (b)	1948 (c)	1949
Cereals		20·4	20·8	22·1	23·7	24·0	26·3	28·8	29·8
Meat and Meat Products		27·3	27·4	30·9	28·7	28·5	28·1	25·6	29·3
Fats		5·8	6·2	6·2	6·0	6·1	5·8	6·4	8·3
Milk (a)		14·1	15·3	16·0	16·3	16·0	16·6	17·9	19·3
Sugar and Preserves		4·1	5·0	5·7	5·4	5·8	5·8	7·8	8·2
Potatoes (inc. chips)		6·1	6·1	6·0	6·5	7·1	7·6	9·3	9·4
Other Vegetables and Fruit		15·7	15·6	17·0	18·5	19·0	25·1	26·8	25·6
Fish		6·4	6·4	7·7	10·1	11·3	11·0	11·6	9·8
Other Foods		14·3	14·5	15·5	16·4	17·6	18·1	22·8	24·2
Total	105¹	114·2	117·3	127·1	131·6	135·4	144·4	157·0	163·9

(a) Liquid and processed
(b) Average for January-September
(c) Average for year excluding February and March

¹ Average expenditure per head on food consumed in the home. Ministry of Labour Budgets 1937–38

FOOD SUBSIDIES

TABLE 17

AMOUNT OF SUBSIDIES AT END OF THE WAR, 1945

	Current price		Price if not subsidized		Subsidy per unit	
	s.	d.	s.	d.	s.	d.
Bread per 4 lb. loaf		9	1	1		4
Flour per 6 lb.	1	3	1	9¼		6¼
Oatmeal per lb.		3½		5		1½
Meat (home killed) per lb.	1	0¾	1	4½		3¾
Bacon per lb.	1	10½	1	11		½
Potatoes per 7 lb.		7		10¾		3¾
Eggs (large) per doz.	2	0	3	6¼	1	6¼
Eggs (small) per doz.	1	9	3	3¼	1	6¼
Sugar per lb.		4		6		2
Milk per quart		9		10		1
Cheese per lb.	1	1	1	4		3
Tea per lb.	2	10	3	0		2

Source. House of Commons statement, 1 June 1945.

TABLE 18

ESTIMATED SUBSIDIES ON FOODSTUFFS FOR YEAR 1950–51

	Current average retail price		Price if not subsidized		Subsidy per unit	
	s.	d.	s.	d.	s.	d.
Bread per 3½ lb. loaf		11	1	5¼		6¼
Flour per 7 lb.	1	9	2	10¾	1	1¾
Carcase meat per lb.	1	5	1	7		2
Bacon per lb.	2	7	3	6½		11½
Potatoes per 7 lb.		10½	1	0½		2
Shell eggs per doz.	3	5¼	4	6¾	1	1½
Sugar per lb.		5		6		1
Milk per quart		10	1	1		3
Cheese per lb.	1	2	1	11½		9½
Tea per lb.	3	4	4	2½		10½
Butter per lb.	2	0	3	0	1	0
Margarine per lb.		10	1	2½		4½
Lard and cooking fat per lb.	1	0	1	3½		3½

Source. Ministry of Food Bulletin.

TABLE 19

NET ANNUAL COST OF FOOD SUBSIDIES
BORNE BY THE MINISTRY OF FOOD DURING THE WAR YEARS

£ million

	1939-40	1940-41	1941-42	1942-43	1943-44	1944-45
Flour, Bread, Oatmeal	10·2	31·8	38·1	34·0	52·2	47·8
Meat	5·5	18·5	19·6	20·5	16·2	19·8
Bacon	0·7	6·5	—	2·1	1·7	1·6
Potatoes	—	0·2	14·4	23·5	16·3	12·0
Eggs and Egg Products	—	—0·5	7·2	14·0	13·9	14·8
Sugar	—4·2	—	3·4	16·3	10·2	15·9
Milk	2·6	3·6	3·2	10·8	11·5	17·4
Milk Schemes	—	7·8	14·4	17·6	20·6	19·9
Milk Products	—0·6	—0·1	—0·3	4·8	9·1	9·1
Other Foods	—1·0	—2·7	—4·3	—1·0	0·1	10·1
Total	13·2	63·1	95·7	142·6	151·8	168·4

Source. *How Britain was Fed in Wartime.*

TABLE 20

SUBSIDIES ON FOODSTUFFS (ESTIMATED)

	1950–51 £ million
Bacon	42·5
Bread and flour	86·6
Shell eggs	31·9
Meat	33·8
Milk	73·2
Butter	43·5
Cheese	16·3
Margarine (domestic)	11·2
Lard and cooking fat	5·0
Potatoes (including acreage payments)	12·6
Sugar (domestic)	7·9
Tea	16·4
Miscellaneous (credit)	27·3
	353·6
Welfare and Milk-in-Schools Schemes	35·7
Fertilizers	11
	400·3
Estimated Total in 1949–50	424·8
Actual Total in 1948–49	484·4

NATIONAL EXPENDITURE ON FOOD

TABLE 21

PERSONAL EXPENDITURE IN THE U.K.

	1938 £m.	Per cent of total	1947 £m.	Per cent of total	1948 £m.	Per cent of total	1949 £m.	Per cent of total
Food—household	1,189	27·6	1,806	24·0	1,964	24·2	2,112	25·1
Food—other	116	2·7	242	3·2	257	3·2	269	3·2
	1,305	30·3	2,048	27·2	2,221	27·4	2,381	28·3
Alcoholic beverages and tobacco	462	10·7	1,369	18·2	1,535	18·9	1,483	17·7
Rent, rates, fuel and light	688	16·0	888	11·8	937	11·6	962	11·4
Household goods	288	6·7	466	6·2	518	6·4	575	6·8
Clothing	446	10·4	704	9·4	853	10·5	948	11·3
Travel and private motoring	290	6·7	425	5·7	421	5·2	443	5·3
Books, etc., communication, entertainment and other goods and services	825	19·2	1,613	21·5	1,623	20·0	1,610	19·2
	4,304	100·0	7,513	100·0	8,108	100·0	8,402	100·0

Source Cmd. 7933. Table 21.
Note. In the item "Other Food", supplies to caterers are valued at the prices paid by the caterers and not at those paid by the final consumer. Therefore when considering personal expenditure from the point of view of the individual, it must be remembered that the other components of the price paid by the consumer appear under other headings such as rent and fuel.

TABLE 22

NATIONAL COST OF CONSUMERS' GOODS AND SERVICES £m.

	1938	1946	1947	1948	1949
Food	1,267	1,993	2,317	2,577	2,748
Total (all goods and services)	3,725	5,632	6,225	6,644	6,962

Source. Cmd. 7933. Table 24.

COMMUNAL FEEDING

TABLE 23

NUMBER OF CANTEENS IN GREAT BRITAIN

Year	Factories employing over 250	Under 250	Total	Docks	Building Sites
1941	3,161	2,530	5,695	110	787
1942	4,340	4,141	8,481	160	868
1943	4,873	5,704	10,577	176	782
1944	5,046	6,584	11,630	179	245
1945	4,883[1]	6,862	11,695	180	179
1946	4,599	7,507	12,106	—	—
1947	4,666	8,569	13,235	—	—
1948	4,835	9,882	14,717	—	—

Source. Annual Reports of the Chief Inspector of Factories.
[1] Decrease due to decrease in number of large factories, not to closing of canteens.

FEEDING OF SCHOOL CHILDREN

TABLE 24

SCHOOL MEALS
NUMBER OF SCHOOL CHILDREN HAVING MEALS ON A
NORMAL DAY IN PRIMARY AND SECONDARY SCHOOLS
ENGLAND AND WALES

	Dinners Thousands	Breakfasts and teas Thousands	Total Thousands
1938–9	150	10	160
1940 July	130	10	140
1941 Feb.	279	5	284
1942 ,,	607	5	612
1943 ,,	1,048	13	1,061
1944 ,,	1,495	20	1,515
1945 ,,	1,650	17	1,667
1946 ,,	1,898	21	1,919
1947 ,,	2,173	22	2,195
1948 ,,	2,598	23	2,621

Notes. Figures relate to public elementary and grant-aided secondary
schools as understood before April 1945. From 1943 Junior Technical Schools are included. Nursery Schools are included from
June 1945. Special Schools are excluded.
Meals served to boarders are excluded.
The figures for 1938–39 and 1940 are estimates and relate to public
elementary schools only.

TABLE 25

SUPPLY OF MILK TO SCHOOL CHILDREN ENGLAND AND WALES

	Number having Milk Thousands	Per cent of no. present %
1938–39	2,500	55
1941 Feb.	2,479	57·6
1942	3,386	77·9
1943	3,371	76·8
1944	3,428	76·3
1945	3,265	73·0
1946	3,269	71·5
1947	3,817	87·0
1948	4,366	87·8

Note. Figures for 1938–39 and 1940 are estimates.
Source. Report to the Food and Agriculture Organization by the United Kingdom for 1947–48.

TABLE 26

COMPARISON OF RETAIL PRICES OF CERTAIN FOODSTUFFS

	1920 1 Nov.		1938 1 Nov.		1947 1 Nov.	
	s.	d.	s.	d.	s.	d.
Beef: British ribs lb.	2	0¾	1	2½	1	3¾
Bread 4 lb.	1	4		8½		9 (3½ lb.)
Sugar (granulated) lb.	1	2		2½		3
Milk, quart		9¾		7		10
Potatoes 7 lb.		11¾		5½		9 or 10d.
Margarine lb.	1	1¾		6½		9
Cheese lb.	1	9		10¾		10

A BRITISH EXAMPLE OF DIFFERENTIAL RATIONING

TABLE 27

VALUE OF BREAD COUPONS IN TERMS OF BREAD

(Bread was unrationed all through the war,
rationing being introduced in 1946 and removed in 1948)

		Manual Worker (man) under 18	19 oz. a day
Normal Adult	9 oz. a day	(woman) ,, ,,	15 ,, ,,
Child under 4	5 ,, ,,	(man)	15 ,, ,,
Child 4 to 11	9 ,, ,,	(woman)	11 ,, ,,
Adolescent 11 to 18	13 ,, ,,		
Expectant Mother	11 ,, ,,		

THE MINISTRY OF FOOD

TABLE 28

MINISTRY OF FOOD EXPENDITURE ON TRADING SERVICES

	1946–47	1947–48	1950–51
	£m.	£m.	£m.
Animal Feeding Stuffs	—	27·6	0·8
Bacon and Ham	3·5	16·1	38·9
Cereals, including cereal feeding stuffs	64·3	127·5	73·1
Eggs and Egg Products	38·1	9·1	32·1
Meat and Livestock	Cr. 5·6	64·6	Cr. 11·7
Milk, including Milk Welfare Schemes	58·3	59·7	99·5
Milk Products	28·0	38·4	40·3
Oils and Fats	—	28·0	Cr. 3·2
Potatoes and Carrots	14·1	7·6	1·7
Sugar	24·1	27·9	Cr. 8·3
Tea	Cr. 8·5	12·7	13·2
Transport, Warehousing and Ancillary Services	17·5	19·7	
Unallocated	—	10·0	—
Contribution towards New Zealand Subsidies	4·0	4·0	
Miscellaneous	6·7	Cr. 19·6	Cr. 10·8
Net Expenditure	244·5	433·3	265·7
Add—Receipts from Sales	999·1	1,091·2	1,285·0
Gross Expenditure	1,243·7	1,524·6	1,550·7

TABLE 29

ANNUAL EXPENDITURE, MINISTRY OF FOOD

	1946–47 £m.	1947–48 £m.	1950–51 £m.
Salaries, travelling exp. etc.	12·8	13·8	11·1
Trading Services (net)	244·5	433·3	265·7
Payments to British Sugar Corporation, Ltd.	2·7	0·6	2·1
Advertising and Publicity	0·5	0·4	0·2
War-time Meals and Emergency Services	0·5	0·3	1·2
Prevention of Food Infestation	—	0·1	—
Contribution to F.A.O.	0·2	0·1	0·5
Groundnuts production in East and Central Africa	0·5	5·7	—
Miscellaneous expenses	0·1	0·6	0·6
Gross Totals	261·7	455·0	281·3
Appropriations in Aid	0·8	7·0	0·3
Net Totals	260·9	448·0	281·0

TABLE 30

REGIONAL IMPORTS BY VALUE OF FOOD AND FEEDINGSTUFFS (f.o.b.)

(Percentages in brackets) £ million

	1946		1947		1948		1949		1950	
Dollar area	189	(36)	241	(34)	141	(17)	168	(19)	157	(16)
Other W. Hemisphere	70	(13)	117	(16)	130	(16)	63	(7)	93	(10)
O.E.E.C. countries	48	(9)	79	(11)	115	(14)	189	(21)	228	(24)
Other non-sterling	14	(3)	21	(3)	65	(8)	61	(7)	71	(7)
Rest of sterling area	199	(38)	261	(36)	375	(45)	427	(47)	410	(43)
Total	520	(100)	719	(100)	826	(100)	908	(100)	959	(100)

Source. *United Kingdom Balance of Payments, 1946 to 1950.* Cmd. 8201.

TABLE 31

FOOD PRODUCTION BY REGIONS. MILLION METRIC TONS

	Far East		N. America		Europe		Latin America		Africa		Oceania		Near East	
	Pre-war	1949	Pre-war	1949	Pre-war	1949	Pre-war	1949	Pre-war	1949	Pre-war	1949	Pre-war	1949
Bread grains	34·8	34·4	27·8	41·9	61·4	58·1	8·9	8·4	2·5	2·8	4·4	6·0	8·5	6·8
Coarse grains	28·8	28·8	78·5	118·1	54·8	49·7	19·8	15·8	6·8	8·6	0·8	1·3	7·0	6·5
Rice (paddy)	142·4	136·0	1·0	1·8	1·1	1·0	2·0	4·4	1·5	1·8	0·1	0·1	1·3	2·0
Sugar	7·3	6·4	1·7	2·0	6·5	6·6	7·6	12·0	1·0	1·3	1·8	2·0	0·2	0·4
Potatoes	7·9	9·8	11·9	13·4	134·7	113·3	2·9	4·4	0·6	0·8	0·5	0·7	0·3	0·9
Fats and oils (vegetable)	8·6	8·1	1·2	2·5	1·0	1·3	1·1	1·0	1·4	1·6	0·2	0·2	0·3	0·4

SELECTED BIBLIOGRAPHY

Official Publications

Food Consumption Levels in the United States, Canada and the United Kingdom. H.M.S.O. 1944. First Report. Second Report. U.S. Dept. of Agriculture 1944. Third Report. U.S. Dept. of Agriculture 1946.

Food Consumption Levels in Australia and the United Kingdom. Canberra 1945.

Food Consumption Levels in the United Kingdom. H.M.S.O. Cmd. 7203. 1947.

Food Consumption Levels in the United Kingdom. H.M.S.O. Cmd. 7842. 1949.

Statistics Relating the War Effort of the United Kingdom. Cmd. 6564. 1944.

The World Food Shortage. 1946. Cmd. 6785.

Second Review of the World Food Shortage. July 1946. Cmd. 6879.

How Britain was Fed in War Time. Food Control 1939–45. H.M.S.O. 1946.

Interim Reports of the Cost of Living Advisory Committee. Cmd. 7077. 1947, Cmd. 8328. 1951, and Cmd. 8481. 1952.

Interim Index of Retail Prices. Method of Construction and Calculation. H.M.S.O. 1950.

Report to the Food and Agricultural Organization by the United Kingdom for 1947–48. H.M.S.O. 1948.

Agricultural Statistics. United Kingdom. H.M.S.O.

Nutritive Values of Wartime Foods. Medical Research Council War Memorandum No. 14. 1945. H.M.S.O.

Economic Survey for 1949. Cmd. 7647.

Economic Survey for 1950. Cmd. 7915.

Economic Survey for 1951. Cmd. 8195.

Monthly Digest of Statistics. H.M.S.O.

Colonial Development Corporation. Reports and Accounts. H.M.S.O.

The Colombo Plan for Co-operative Economic Development in South and South-East Asia. Cmd. 8080. 1950.

Ministry of Food Bulletin. Jan. 1950 onwards.

Consumption of Food in the United States. 1909–18. U.S. Dept. of Agriculture. 1949.

Widdowson, E. M. *A Study of Individual Children's Diets.* Medical Research Council. H.M.S.O. 1947.

Hancock, W. K. and Gowing, M. M. *British War Economy.* H.M.S.O. 1949.

National Income and Expenditure of the United Kingdom, 1938 to 1946. Cmd. 7099.

National Income and Expenditure of the United Kingdom, 1946 to 1950. Cmd. 8203.

A Plan for the Mechanized Production of Groundnuts in East and Central Africa. 1947. Cmd. 7030.

East African Groundnuts Scheme. Review of Progress. 1948. Cmd. 7314.

The Future of the Overseas Food Corporation. 1951. Cmd. 8125.

Reports, etc.

Recommended Dietary Allowances. National Research Council, Washington, D.C. 1945.
Final Report on Nutrition of the Mixed Committee of League of Nations. 1937.
Bulletin of the Oxford University Institute of Statistics. Various articles by T. Schultz.
Wartime Rationing and Consumption. Economic Intelligence Service. League of Nations, 1942.
British Medical Association. *Report of the Committee on Nutrition.* 1950.
British Association. *Reports* 1881 *and* 1882.

Surveys

City and County of Newcastle-upon-Tyne. *A Study of Diets of Sixty-nine Working-Class Families in Newcastle-on-Tyne.* 1936.
County Council of West Riding of Yorkshire. *Report on a Study of Diets of 205 Families in the West Riding of Yorkshire.* 1939.
Crawford, W. and Broadley, H. *The People's Food.* London, 1938.
Ford, P. *Work and Wealth in a Modern Port.* London, 1934.
Jones, D. Caradog. *The Social Survey of Merseyside.* London, 1934.
Murray, K. A. H. and Rutherford, R. S. G. *Milk Consumption Habits, 1941.*
New Survey of London Life and Labour. 1932.
Orr, J. B. *Food, Health and Income.* 1936.
Rowntree, B. S. *Poverty and Progress.* A Second Social Survey of York. 1941.

F.A.O. Reports

Handbook for the Preparation of Food Balance Sheets. 1949.
World Food Survey. 1946.
Food and Agricultural Statistics. Monthly Bulletin.
World Food Appraisal as of April, 1949.
Reports of the Council of F.A.O.
Reports of the Sessions of the Conferences.
National Progress in Food and Agriculture Programmes. 1948.
The State of Food and Agriculture, 1948 and 1949.
Teaching Better Nutrition, 1950. (F.A.O. Nutritional Studies, No. 6).

Books and Articles

Ashley, W. *The Bread of our Forefathers.* 1926.
Astor and Rowntree. *British Agriculture.* 1939.
Bacharach, A. L. and Rendle, T. (Edited.) *The Nation's Food.*
Beveridge, W. *British Food Control.* 1928.
Blitz, J. F. *Behind the Ration Book.* 1950.
Clark, F. Le Gros. *Feeding the Human Family.* 1947.

Curtis-Bennett, N. *The Food of the People. The History of Industrial Feeding.* 1949.

Davies, David. *The Case of Labourers in Husbandry Stated and Considered.* 1795.

Drummond, J. and Wilbraham, A. *The Englishman's Food To-day.* 1939.

Eden, F. *State of the Poor.* 1797.

Fenelon, K. G. *Measuring Britain's Food.* 1949. Economics I, Part 1.

Fenelon, K. G. *Britain's Food Supplies.* 1950. Advancement of Science, 24, 311.

Fenelon, K. G. *The World's Food Supplies.* 1951. Advancement of Science. 29, 38.

Hammond, R. J. *Food.* Vol. I., *The Growth of Policy,* 1951.

Kitchin, A. H. and Passmore R. *The Scotsman's Food.* 1949.

Leitch, I. *The Evolution of Dietary Standards.* 1941–42. Nutrition Abstracts and Reviews, 502.

Marrack, J. *Food and Planning.* 1946.

Plimmer, R. and V. *Food, Health and Vitamins.*

Pyke, Magnus. *Industrial Nutrition.* 1950.

Russell, Sir John. Presidential Address. British Association. Newcastle Meeting. 1949.

Smith, C. *Britain's Food Supplies in Peace and War.*

Yates, P. L. and Warriner, D. *Food and Farming in Post-War Europe.*

Index

Printed in the United States
by Baker & Taylor Publisher Services